MODERNIZING CRIMINAL JUSTICE

Modernizing Criminal Justice

LOK SABHA INITIATIVES

Mack Rafeal

Mohammed Altaf Hussain

Contents

Table of Content

Introduction

Introduction

Modernizing the law enforcement framework is a basic endeavor for any general public endeavoring to guarantee decency, effectiveness, and responsiveness. With regards to India, the Lok Sabha, the lower place of the Parliament, has been at the front of drives pointed toward introducing exhaustive changes to address the difficulties and inadequacies of the current law enforcement structure. The requirement for modernization emerges from an intersection of elements, including innovative headways, changing cultural elements, and a developing comprehension of equity. This presentation dives into the different features of the modernization drives embraced by the Lok Sabha in the domain of law enforcement, investigating the key drivers, difficulties, and possible results of these groundbreaking endeavors.

At the core of the Lok Sabha's modernization plan lies an acknowledgment of the diverse idea of the difficulties facing the law enforcement framework in India. The current system, established in pioneer period regulations and methods, has frequently been studied for its laziness, absence of straightforwardness, and inability to stay up with contemporary requests. The coming of the computerized age has additionally highlighted the need for a change in perspective, provoking legislators to reevaluate conventional methodologies for additional coordinated and mechanically complex arrangements.

One of the urgent parts of the Lok Sabha's drives in modernizing law enforcement is the undertaking to upgrade the analytical and legal abilities of policing. The conventional techniques for wrongdoing identification and proof social event are being expanded and, now and again, supplanted by state of the art advances. The coordination of man-made reasoning (simulated intelligence), AI, and information examination into criminal examinations is a demonstration of the Lok Sabha's obligation to utilizing innovation for more viable policing.

Furthermore, the Lok Sabha has perceived the requirement for lawful changes to smooth out and assist the settlement interaction. Redesiging obsolete rules, changing procedural regulations, and presenting elective question goal systems are essential parts of this modernization drive. The point isn't just to diminish the overabundance of cases yet in addition to guarantee that equity is conveyed on time, lining up with the protected command of a quick and fair preliminary.

Moreover, the Lok Sabha's modernization drives reach out past the court and the police headquarters to include remedial offices and recovery programs. Perceiving the meaning of detainee reconstruction and reintegration into society, regulative measures have been acquainted with patch up the jail framework.

The accentuation is on establishing a rehabilitative climate that works with the reintegration of guilty parties into standard society, consequently tending to the main drivers of criminal way of behaving.

In any case, the way to modernization is full of difficulties, and the Lok Sabha's drives are not without their faultfinders. One significant obstacle is the need to work out some kind of harmony between innovative progressions and protecting individual privileges and security. The utilization of reconnaissance advances, biometrics, and information examination in criminal examinations raises worries about possible encroachments on common freedoms. The Lok Sabha should explore these worries cautiously, guaranteeing that the reception of innovation is joined by hearty lawful shields and oversight systems.

Besides, the financial incongruities inside the Indian populace represent a test to the impartial execution of modernization drives. Admittance to innovation, lawful portrayal, and training fluctuates broadly across various fragments of society. The Lok Sabha should address these inconsistencies to forestall the worsening of existing disparities inside the law enforcement framework. In doing as such, the modernization endeavors can be really comprehensive, helping all residents regardless of their financial foundation.

One more basic part of the modernization plan is the requirement for limit working inside the policing legal apparatus. The presentation of new innovations and methodology requires exhaustive preparation projects to guarantee that partners are prepared to explore the advancing scene of law enforcement. The Lok Sabha's drives must, subsequently, incorporate arrangements for preparing and expertise advancement to engage the labor force and improve their capacities in taking care of present day apparatuses and strategies.

Regardless of these difficulties, the Lok Sabha's modernization drives hold the commitment of extensive advantages for the law enforcement framework and society at large. The combination of innovation is supposed to improve the exactness and effectiveness of criminal examinations, decreasing the probability of unjust convictions and guaranteeing that the liable are dealt with. Besides, the straightforwardness managed by modernization measures can add to reconstructing public confidence in the law enforcement framework, a vital consider encouraging an amicable and reputable society.

Pair with mechanical progressions, the Lok Sabha's drives additionally accentuate the significance of local area commitment and partner cooperation in the law enforcement process. Perceiving that equity isn't exclusively the domain of policing the legal executive, endeavors are being made to include the local area in wrongdoing counteraction, casualty backing, and restoration drives. This people group driven approach lines up with the standards of helpful equity, looking to fix the mischief brought about by criminal way of behaving and reintegrate people into their networks.

Moreover, the Lok Sabha's modernization plan stretches out to global coordinated efforts and associations. Perceiving that numerous crimes rise above public boundaries, the drives remember arrangements for collaboration with different nations for regions, for example, data sharing, removal, and joint examination endeavors. This worldwide point of view mirrors a comprehension of the interconnected idea of present day wrongdoing and the need for an organized reaction at the global level.

1. **Overview of the current state of the criminal justice system in India**

   The present status of the law enforcement framework in India is set apart by a complicated transaction of verifiable heritages, financial difficulties, and institutional elements. As the world's biggest majority rules government, India's law enforcement framework is entrusted with keeping up with the rule of law, guaranteeing equity for casualties, and maintaining the freedoms of the denounced. Notwithstanding, a nuanced comprehension of its assets and shortcomings uncovers a framework wrestling with a heap of issues that hinder its viability and decency.

   One of the essential difficulties confronting the Indian law enforcement framework is the sheer volume of cases and the subsequent overabundance. Throughout the long term, a huge gathering of cases has happened, prompting delayed preliminary cycles and deferred equity. The accumulation is especially intense in lower courts, where most of cases are started. This postponement not just sabotages the guideline of quick equity revered in the Indian Constitution yet in addition puts an unjustifiable weight on the blamed, casualties, and witnesses.

   The build-up is exacerbated by the deficiency of legal framework and labor supply. The proportion of judges to the populace in India is altogether settle for what is most convenient option, adding to the sluggish speed of preliminaries. The deficiency of judges, combined with obsolete court strategies, enhances the difficulties of case removal. Endeavors to resolve this issue, like the arrangement of extra appointed authorities and the foundation of new courts, have been started, yet the size of the issue requires maintained and extensive changes.

Intensifying these difficulties are obsolete legitimate arrangements and procedural intricacies that thwart the productive regulation of equity. Numerous regulations in India are leftovers of the frontier period, and their pertinence in the contemporary setting has been addressed. The intricacy of legitimate cycles and the unpredictable trap of old regulations add to disarray and deferrals. The requirement for an orderly survey and redesign of these regulations is broadly recognized, and inconsistent endeavors have been made to change and refresh explicit resolutions. Be that as it may, a complete and comprehensive methodology is fundamental to smooth out the legitimate structure and make it more open and receptive to the requirements of contemporary society.

One more basic feature of the present status of the law enforcement framework in India is the financial abberations that penetrate each phase of the legitimate cycle.

Admittance to legitimate portrayal, a major right ensured by the Constitution, stays a test for underestimated and monetarily hindered segments of society. The powerlessness to manage the cost of capable legitimate insight frequently leaves people in a difficult spot, undermining their capacity to introduce a hearty safeguard. This lopsidedness is additionally exacerbated by the absence of mindfulness about legitimate privileges and systems, especially in rustic regions, where a critical piece of the populace lives.

The predicament of undertrials is a glaring sign of the financial variations inside the law enforcement framework. A significant level of the jail populace in India contains people who are anticipating preliminary, large numbers of whom are financially impeded and unfit to get bail. The delayed confinement of undertrials, once in a while surpassing the likely sentence for the supposed offense, not just disregards the standard of "free and clear by default" yet in addition adds to jail stuffing.

Jail conditions in India present one more element of worry inside the law enforcement framework. Packed jails, insufficient offices, and an absence of recovery programs portray the condition of restorative foundations. The goal of jails ought to reach out past discipline to incorporate the restoration and renewal of prisoners. Nonetheless, the overall circumstances in numerous Indian penitentiaries miss the mark concerning worldwide guidelines, presenting difficulties to the effective reintegration of wrongdoers into society.

Moreover, the connection between policing and the networks they serve is much of the time stressed, mirroring a more extensive issue of trust shortage. Occasions of police wrongdoing, erratic captures, and custodial viciousness have been accounted for, disintegrating public trust in the law enforcement framework. Building a relationship of trust between policing the local area is fundamental for viable wrongdoing counteraction and guaranteeing the collaboration of residents in the analytical cycle.

The utilization of innovation in the law enforcement framework is another perspective that warrants consideration. While there have been endeavors to present mechanical answers for case the board, proof assortment, and correspondence, the speed of reception changes across various states and areas. The advanced gap, restricted foundation, and the requirement for thorough preparation frustrate the broad execution of innovation, restricting its capability to improve the productivity and straightforwardness of the law enforcement process.

In the domain of criminology, the present status of issues uncovers a requirement for huge improvement. Criminological proof assumes a significant part in criminal examinations and court procedures. Be that as it may, the limit of scientific research centers, the nature of criminological examination, and the joining of measurable discoveries into legal procedures require upgrade. Reinforcing legal abilities is vital to guaranteeing precise and dependable proof, consequently adding to the believability of the law enforcement framework.

Regardless of these difficulties, it is fundamental to perceive the positive steps and drives that have been attempted to further develop the law enforcement framework in India. The foundation of particular courts, for example, quick track courts for explicit offenses and devoted courts for cases including youngsters, mirrors a promise to speedy and specific equity. Furthermore, the presentation of elective debate goal components, including intervention and request bartering, looks to ease the weight on customary courts and work with speedier goals.

Lately, there has been a developing affirmation of the significance of casualty driven approaches inside the law enforcement framework. Drives to offer help administrations for casualties, safeguard their freedoms, and improve their support in legal procedures are positive developments. Perceiving casualties as key partners in the equity cycle is a huge shift that lines up with global prescribed procedures.

The development of lawful guide administrations and the advancement of legitimate education programs are estimable endeavors to resolve the issue of admittance to equity, particularly for underestimated networks. These drives plan to engage people with information about their legitimate freedoms and privileges, crossing over the data hole and cultivating a more comprehensive lawful scene.

2. Importance of modernization for effective and fair law enforcement

Modernization is a basic part of guaranteeing powerful and fair policing contemporary social orders. The scene of policing gone through massive changes throughout the long term, driven by mechanical headways, developing cultural necessities, and a more profound comprehension of equity. Embracing modernization isn't simply a question of staying up with the times; it is an essential necessity for policing to satisfy their command of keeping public control, forestalling and examining violations, and maintaining the standards of equity. In this sweeping conversation, we investigate the complex significance of modernization for policing, upon mechanical combination, procedural proficiency, local area commitment, and the security of individual freedoms.

Mechanical headways assume a vital part in improving the capacities of policing. The reconciliation of state of the art advances like computerized reasoning (man-made intelligence), AI, information examination, and biometrics has reformed the insightful and wrongdoing avoidance processes. These devices engage policing filter through immense measures of information, distinguish designs, and foresee expected crimes. For instance, prescient policing calculations dissect authentic wrongdoing information to distinguish areas of interest and patterns, permitting policing designate assets decisively and proactively address arising dangers.

Also, current advances add to the exactness and effectiveness of criminal examinations. DNA investigation, legal advances, and computerized proof assessment have become key apparatuses in settling complex cases.

These progressions help in recognizing culprits as well as assume a critical part in excusing the honest. The utilization of body-worn cameras by cops gives an extra layer of responsibility and straightforwardness, catching continuous cooperations and filling in as significant proof in examinations.

The dependence on innovation likewise stretches out to the domain of correspondence and data sharing. Policing can now team up consistently across locales, sharing basic data and knowledge to battle transnational wrongdoing and psychological oppression. The appearance of interconnected data sets and secure correspondence channels works with quick and composed reactions to arising dangers, supporting the worldwide idea of contemporary crimes.

Proficiency in policing is one more convincing justification behind modernization. The customary strategies for manual record-keeping, case the board, and correspondence are innately tedious and inclined to blunders. Modernization smoothes out these cycles, lessening regulatory bottlenecks and speeding up the progression of data inside policing. Electronic case the board frameworks, robotized record-keeping, and computerized correspondence stages upgrade the proficiency of managerial errands, permitting policing to zero in more on proactive policing and wrongdoing anticipation.

Besides, modernization adds to the speedy goal of legitimate cases. The joining of innovation into court procedures, for example, e-documenting frameworks, video conferencing for hearings, and electronic proof show, speeds up the legal interaction. This is especially critical in resolving the issue of case build-up, a longstanding test in numerous overall sets of laws. Quick settlement not just guarantees convenient equity for casualties and the charged yet additionally fills in as an obstruction by showing the outcomes of criminal conduct in a more prompt style.

A fair and powerful policing requires a harmony between wrongdoing control and the security of individual freedoms. Modernization tries can assume a urgent part in accomplishing this fragile harmony. For example, the utilization of body-worn cameras supports gathering proof as well as advances responsibility by catching the activities and connections of policemen. This straightforwardness helps in encouraging public trust and considers both policing residents responsible for their direct.

Moreover, modernization takes into consideration the joining of shields to safeguard individual security privileges. As innovation propels, so do worries about the likely abuse of observation instruments. Officials and policing should work cooperatively to lay out powerful lawful structures that oversee the moral utilization of observation advances, guaranteeing that they are sent in a way that regards individual protection and common freedoms.

Biometric advances, like finger impression and facial acknowledgment frameworks, are amazing assets for policing, in the distinguishing proof and misgiving of suspects.

Nonetheless, their arrangement should be joined by clear strategies and shields to forestall abuse and safeguard against outlandish interruption into individual security. The foundation of rigid conventions for the assortment, stockpiling, and sharing of biometric information is essential to figure out some kind of harmony between compelling policing shielding individual freedoms.

Local area commitment is an indispensable part of present day policing. Building trust and cooperation between policing and the networks they serve is fundamental for keeping public control and forestalling wrongdoing. Modernization drives that focus on local area policing, exchange, and straightforwardness add to a positive connection between policemen and people in general. Drawing in with the local area not just aides in recognizing and tending to nearby worries yet in addition cultivates a feeling of shared liability regarding public security.

Also, modernization takes into consideration the execution of local area arranged projects and drives that go past conventional policing. Cooperative endeavors to resolve social issues, for example, substance misuse, psychological wellness, and youth commitment can add to wrongdoing anticipation and the general prosperity of networks. By embracing a comprehensive methodology that considers the main drivers of criminal way of behaving, policing become impetuses for positive social change.

With regards to worldwide participation, modernization is vital for tending to the difficulties presented by transnational wrongdoing. Crimes, including cybercrime, illegal exploitation, and psychological warfare, frequently rise above public lines. Viable policing the cutting edge time requires consistent coordinated effort and data dividing among nations. Worldwide data sets, joint teams, and normalized conventions for removal and legitimate collaboration are fundamental parts of a modernized way to deal with battling worldwide wrongdoing organizations.

Besides, modernization adds to the versatile limit of policing the substance of arising dangers. The idea of wrongdoing develops with cultural changes and mechanical progressions, requiring a proactive and dynamic methodology. Policing that embrace modernization are better prepared to answer new and complex difficulties, for example, digital dangers, computerized extortion, and the utilization of innovation by crooks to sidestep location. Nonstop preparation and ability improvement programs are fundamental to guarantee that policing stay capable at exploring the developing scene of crimes.

3. Role of Lok Sabha in initiating reforms

The Lok Sabha, as the lower place of India's Parliament, assumes an essential part in starting and controlling regulative changes that shape the socio-political and monetary scene of the country.

The Lok Sabha, comprising of straightforwardly chosen delegates of individuals, is at the front of administrative navigation, and its drives frequently mirror the yearnings, concerns, and formative necessities of the different Indian people. In this far reaching investigation, we dig into the multi-layered job of the Lok Sabha in starting changes, taking into account its administrative capabilities, oversight obligations, and its job in forming the arrangement plan of the country.

Administrative Capabilities:

At the center of the Lok Sabha's job in starting changes is its essential capability as a regulative body. The Lok Sabha, alongside the Rajya Sabha (the upper house), is liable for passing regulations, correcting existing resolutions, and resolving basic issues that require an official reaction. The Lok Sabha's regulative plan is different, covering regions like financial approaches, social government assistance, instruction, wellbeing, foundation, and that's just the beginning.

The commencement of changes frequently begins with the presentation of bills in the Lok Sabha. Individuals from Parliament (MPs) propose bills to address arising difficulties, amend regulative holes, or present new strategies lined up with the changing necessities of society. These bills can be government bills, mirroring the needs of the decision party, or confidential individuals' bills, mirroring the points of view of individual MPs regardless of party association.

The Lok Sabha's part in examining, discussing, and at last passing or dismissing these bills is a pivotal part of its regulative capabilities. The deliberative interaction takes into consideration different perspectives to be thought of, cultivating a powerful and majority rule dynamic climate. The section of regulation mirrors the aggregate will of the Lok Sabha, connoting its responsiveness to the advancing requirements of the country.

Oversight and Responsibility:

Aside from its official capabilities, the Lok Sabha fills in as a gathering for oversight and responsibility. Through different parliamentary councils, the Lok Sabha audits the working of various government divisions and organizations, guaranteeing that they are executing arrangements successfully and using dispensed assets sensibly. These boards, like the Public Records Panel (PAC) and the Evaluations Council, assume a basic part in examining government activities, uses, and the general execution of strategies.

Oversight by the Lok Sabha adds to straightforwardness and responsibility in administration. It empowers MPs to address government authorities, request clarifications for strategy disappointments or slips by, and consider the leader responsible for its activities. This oversight capability is especially huge with regards to changes, as it guarantees that the expected objectives of administrative drives are accomplished and that the public authority is considered answerable for the results.

Strategy Definition and Plan Setting:

The Lok Sabha, being a delegate body, is instrumental in forming the strategy plan of the country. Through discussions, conversations, and the section of goals, the Lok Sabha explains the needs and worries of the Indian public. It fills in as a stage for MPs to advocate for explicit strategies, changes, or changes in existing regulations in view of how they might interpret the necessities of their voting public.

In addition, the Lok Sabha mirrors the political will of the decision party or alliance. The arrangements and changes supported by the decision party are many times reflected in the regulative plan of the Lok Sabha. The yearly spending plan, introduced by the public authority in the Lok Sabha, frames the monetary portions for different areas and projects, demonstrating the organization's arrangement needs and reformative measures.

The Lok Sabha's part in strategy detailing stretches out past the authoritative cycle. Its discussions, question meetings, and conversations on issues of public significance add to the forming of popular assessment. The explanation of different perspectives inside the Lok Sabha mirrors the vote based ethos of the country, guaranteeing that strategy choices are educated by a wide range regarding viewpoints.

Protected Changes and Central Changes:

The Lok Sabha holds an unmistakable job in starting sacred changes, a cycle that can prompt crucial changes in the administration structure. While sacred changes require an exceptional greater part in the two places of Parliament and endorsement by a larger part of state governing bodies, the Lok Sabha is much of the time the main thrust behind such extraordinary drives.

By and large, the Lok Sabha plays had a focal impact in basic protected revisions. For instance, the 73rd and 74th Corrections in 1992, which decentralized capacity to nearby bodies, were critical changes started to reinforce grassroots administration. Likewise, corrections connected with constituent changes, hostile to absconding regulations, and reservation arrangements have all seen dynamic interest and discussion inside the Lok Sabha.

These protected alterations, frequently incited by changing social elements and the requirement for comprehensive administration, exhibit the Lok Sabha's obligation to adjusting the established structure to contemporary real factors. The ability to change the constitution highlights the Lok Sabha's impact in molding the lawful and institutional underpinnings of the country.

Tending to Social and Financial Differences:

The Lok Sabha is instrumental in tending to social and financial differences through official drives and strategy measures. As the chosen agents of individuals, MPs deliver the worries and desires of their constituents, including those from underestimated and oppressed areas of society. Changes pointed toward tending to differences in training, medical care, business, and admittance to equity are frequently advocated and thought upon in the Lok Sabha.

The presentation and section of governmental policy regarding minorities in society strategies, like bookings for Planned Ranks, Planned Clans, and Other In reverse Classes, have been huge moves toward tending to verifiable shameful acts and social disparities. The Lok Sabha, through its deliberative cycles, has been a vital field for banters on these strategies, mirroring the different suppositions on the most proficient method to accomplish civil rights and value.

In the monetary domain, the Lok Sabha's part in supporting monetary allotments and financial arrangements is essential for driving comprehensive development. Changes connected with tax collection, monetary approaches, and financial improvement methodologies are formed through conversations and discussions inside the Lok Sabha. The accentuation on destitution easing, provincial turn of events, and business age frequently tracks down articulation in the regulative plan of the Lok Sabha, mirroring a guarantee to tending to monetary variations.

Peaceful accords and Coordinated efforts:

The Lok Sabha assumes a part in molding India's worldwide commitment and responsibilities. Settlements, arrangements, and coordinated efforts with different countries frequently require parliamentary endorsement. The Lok Sabha, through its consultations and conversations, investigates these peaceful accords, guaranteeing that they line up with the public premium and stick to protected standards.

The commencement of changes in regions like international strategy, economic accords, and vital partnerships mirrors the Lok Sabha's job in adjusting India's worldwide commitment to changing international real factors. The discussions on global issues inside the Lok Sabha give a stage to MPs to communicate different points of view on India's part on the planet and impact the course of conciliatory and worldwide relations.

Difficulties and Amazing open doors:

While the Lok Sabha holds an essential job in starting changes, it likewise faces difficulties in guaranteeing powerful and comprehensive lawmaking. Political polarization, procedural bottlenecks, and disturbances during meetings can hinder the smooth working of the Lok Sabha. The test of adjusting provincial interests and various perspectives inside the huge and heterogeneous Indian commonwealth requires capable parliamentary initiative and a promise to agreement building.

Open doors for improving the Lok Sabha's job in starting changes lie in utilizing innovation for more comprehensive and participatory administration. E-administration devices, public discussions, and the utilization of information investigation can improve the proficiency and straightforwardness of the regulative cycle. Also, fortifying parliamentary boards of trustees and empowering bipartisan cooperation can add to more educated and nuanced direction.

Chapter 1

Understanding the Challenges

Understanding the difficulties confronting any complicated framework, be it cultural, monetary, or political, is fundamental for significant change and progress. With regards to India, a country set apart by variety, verifiable heritages, and financial intricacies, understanding the difficulties is principal to making successful and comprehensive arrangements. This investigation jumps into the bunch difficulties standing up to India, incorporating monetary inconsistencies, social disparities, administration issues, ecological worries, and international elements.

Financial Inconsistencies and Disparities:

India wrestles with articulated financial inconsistencies that manifest across different aspects. Pay disparity is a squeezing worry, with a huge abundance hole between the well-to-do and the monetarily impeded. Metropolitan rustic partitions worsen these variations, with metropolitan focuses encountering fast monetary development while provincial regions frequently face agrarian trouble and restricted admittance to valuable open doors.

Joblessness and underemployment compound the monetary difficulties, especially among the young. Notwithstanding India's segment profit, the jumble between abilities requested by the gig market and the abilities bestowed through the schooling system prompts a huge piece of the populace being avoided with regard to the conventional labor force.

Moreover, the casual area, which comprises a significant piece of the economy, faces issues like absence of employer stability, insufficient wages, and restricted admittance to government backed retirement measures. Spanning these monetary variations requires a complete methodology that tends to instruction, expertise improvement, work creation, and social wellbeing nets.

Social Imbalances and Segregation:

India's social texture is complicatedly woven with variety, including different positions, religions, dialects, and identities. Nonetheless, this variety is joined by determined social imbalances and segregation. The position framework, in spite of legitimate mediations, keeps on affecting social elements, especially in rustic regions. Oppression minimized networks, including Dalits and ancestral populaces, stays a test, influencing their admittance to schooling, business, and social open doors.

Orientation imbalance is another critical social test. In spite of progress in certain areas, ladies keep on confronting separation, brutality, and restricted admittance to training and business potential open doors. Engaging ladies through schooling, monetary interest, and regulative changes is essential for encouraging a more impartial society.

Strict and shared pressures likewise present difficulties to social amicability. Episodes of strict prejudice and public viciousness highlight the requirement for supported endeavors to advance resistance, interfaith discourse, and regard for variety. Reinforcing social attachment is fundamental for cultivating a comprehensive and amicable society.

Administration Issues and Regulatory Difficulties:

Administration challenges are innate in a huge and various majority rules system like India. Regulatory formality, debasement, and failures in policy implementation frequently ruin the powerful execution of strategies and projects. The conveyance of public administrations, especially in country and far off regions, faces hindrances like deficient framework, absence of assets, and regulatory obstacles.

Decentralization of administration, as conceived in the Panchayati Raj framework, means to address these difficulties by enabling nearby self-government bodies. In any case, the successful execution of decentralization requires defeating obstruction at different levels and guaranteeing that neighborhood bodies have the independence, assets, and ability to satisfy their jobs.

Political polarization and administration challenges likewise manifest at the state and focal levels. The requirement for agreement building, helpful federalism, and a more cooperative methodology between various levels of government is essential for defeating regulatory obstacles and conveying responsive administration.

Ecological Maintainability and Environmental Change:

India faces critical ecological difficulties coming from fast urbanization, industrialization, and populace development. Air and water contamination, deforestation, and the exhaustion of normal assets are basic worries. The outcomes of natural debasement, including medical problems, loss of biodiversity, and unfriendly effects on horticulture, require pressing consideration.

Environmental change represents extra difficulties, with India defenseless against outrageous climate occasions, rising ocean levels, and disturbances to farming examples. Moderating and adjusting to environmental change requires a coordinated exertion, consolidating maintainable improvement rehearses, sustainable power drives, and proactive natural protection measures.

Offsetting monetary improvement with natural manageability is a sensitive errand. Arrangements that advance green innovations, supportable metropolitan preparation, and protection rehearses are fundamental for guaranteeing that financial development doesn't come to the detriment of ecological prosperity.

International Elements and Public safety:

India's international scene is set apart by an intricate trap of associations with adjoining nations and worldwide powers. International difficulties, including line questions, provincial contentions, and international competitions, require conciliatory artfulness and vital policymaking. The security worries in line districts, especially with Pakistan and China, highlight the significance of a hearty public safeguard technique.

Online protection dangers and hilter kilter fighting likewise present difficulties to public safety. Creating complete systems to address arising security dangers, upgrade insight capacities, and reinforce guard framework is pivotal for defending the country's advantages.

Discretion assumes a basic part in exploring global relations. India's essential organizations, support in provincial gatherings, and obligation to a multipolar world request require proficient conciliatory commitment to propel public interests and add to worldwide dependability.

Medical services and General Wellbeing Difficulties:

The Coronavirus pandemic has brought to the front the difficulties inside India's medical services framework. While India has taken huge steps in medical care framework and infectious prevention, there are relentless provokes, for example, lacking admittance to medical services administrations, lopsided dispersion of medical services offices among metropolitan and provincial regions, and a deficiency of medical services experts.

Guaranteeing reasonable and open medical care for all residents is a squeezing challenge. Fortifying essential medical care, putting resources into preventive measures, and tending to differences in medical care access are fundamental parts of medical services change.

Furthermore, tending to wellbeing related difficulties like unhealthiness, sterilization, and maternal wellbeing adds to in general cultural prosperity.

General wellbeing challenges reach out past irresistible infections to issues like emotional well-being, non-transferable sicknesses, and the effect of ecological variables on wellbeing. Extensive general wellbeing arrangements, local area commitment, and interests in medical services research are basic for tending to these difficulties.

Instructive Changes and Ability Improvement:

While India has gained huge headway in growing admittance to schooling, challenges continue guaranteeing quality training, decreasing dropout rates, and crossing over the metropolitan provincial training partition. Abberations in instructive results in light of financial elements and orientation feature the requirement for designated mediations.

Besides, the school system should line up with the requests of the gig market to address the test of joblessness and underemployment. Expertise improvement programs, professional preparation, and drives to encourage development and business are fundamental for furnishing the labor force with the abilities expected in a quickly developing worldwide economy.

Lacking admittance to quality advanced education, especially in country regions, presents difficulties for making a talented and serious labor force. Changes in the schooling area, including educational plan refreshes, computerized learning drives, and innovative work ventures, are essential for setting up the cutting edge for the difficulties and chances of the 21st hundred years.

1.1 Analysis of the existing challenges in the criminal justice system

The law enforcement framework in any general public fills in as the foundation of the rule of law, guaranteeing the fair and only treatment of people engaged with legal procedures. With regards to India, a nation set apart by its variety and intricacy, the law enforcement framework faces a heap of difficulties that effect its viability and reasonableness. This examination investigates the current difficulties inside the Indian law enforcement framework, incorporating issues connected with legitimate structures, policing, remedies, and more extensive financial variables.

Obsolete Lawful Structures:

One of the huge difficulties tormenting the Indian law enforcement framework is the presence of obsolete legitimate structures. Numerous regulations in India have establishes in provincial time regulation, which may not line up with contemporary cultural standards or sufficiently address arising types of crime. The sluggish speed of legitimate changes and the ingenuity of old resolutions frustrate the framework's capacity to adjust to the advancing idea of wrongdoing.

The postpone in refreshing and modernizing legitimate structures makes holes and ambiguities in the law, prompting difficulties in requirement and settlement. Policymakers should focus on far reaching lawful changes to guarantee that the general set of laws stays pertinent, viable, and simply despite changing cultural elements.

Overburdened Legal executive and Overabundance of Cases:

The Indian legal executive faces an impressive test in managing a mind-boggling caseload and a diligent overabundance of cases. The sheer volume of prosecution, combined with procedural deferrals, adds to a drawn out span for the goal of cases. This accumulation not just subverts the rule of quick equity cherished in the Constitution yet additionally brings about the delayed imprisonment of people anticipating preliminary.

Overburdened courts, especially at the lower levels, battle to adapt to the case-load, prompting defers in conveying equity. The issue is intensified by a deficiency of judges, insufficient framework, and procedural intricacies. The requirement for the opportune removal of cases is basic not just for the charged, who are qualified for a quick preliminary, yet in addition for the successful working of the law enforcement framework in general.

Lacking Police Assets and Preparing:

Policing, especially at the state and nearby levels, wrestle with an absence of assets, both human and material. Lacking subsidizing, obsolete gear, and restricted labor supply upset the capacity of the police to forestall and research violations successfully. Lacking preparation and expert advancement programs further trade off the capacities of policemen.

The deficiency of police staff and the resultant weighty responsibility add to examples of exhaustion, stress, and possible wrongdoing. The requirement for interest in modernizing police foundation, giving continuous preparation, and up-grading enlistment endeavors is clear. An exceptional and prepared police force is fundamental for keeping up with the rule of law, leading careful examinations, and guaranteeing public confidence in the law enforcement framework.

Financial Variations and Admittance to Equity:

Admittance to equity is a central rule that ought to be generally accessible, yet financial differences present a huge hindrance in such manner. People from monetarily burdened foundations frequently battle to get to legitimate portrayal, prompting differences in the nature of safeguard in criminal cases. This awkward-ness adds to the insight that the law enforcement framework isn't similarly open to all, sabotaging its authenticity.

The absence of legitimate mindfulness and training, especially in rustic regions, further compounds the difficulties of admittance to equity. Numerous people know nothing about their legitimate privileges or miss the mark on means to successfully affirm them.

Crossing over these financial holes requires designated endeavors to advance lawful proficiency, improve admittance to legitimate guide administrations, and address foundational imbalances that add to abberations in the law enforcement framework.

Jail Congestion and Lacking Restoration:

India's jails wrestle with the test of congestion, a consequence of the great number of undertrials and a sluggish paced legal cycle. Stuffed jails strain assets, compromise the prosperity of detainees, and upset the adequacy of recovery programs. The day to day environments in numerous detainment facilities miss the mark concerning global principles, affecting the physical and emotional wellness of prisoners.

Furthermore, the emphasis on corrective estimates over rehabilitative endeavors adds to the propagation of a pattern of guiltiness. A more far reaching way to deal with revisions is fundamental, stressing the restoration and reintegration of wrong-doers into society. Putting resources into instructive and professional preparation programs inside jail settings can outfit people with the abilities essential for a fruit-ful reintegration upon discharge.

Innovation Holes and Computerized Gap:

While innovation can be a useful asset for upgrading the law enforcement frame-work, there exist huge holes in its execution and openness. Not all policing have the assets or framework to use current advancements for examinations, proof ad-ministration, and case following. This innovation hole can obstruct the proficiency and adequacy of criminal examinations.

Besides, the advanced separation in the nation raises worries about the im-partial utilization of innovation in the law enforcement framework. Abberations in admittance to innovation, especially in country regions, may prompt inconsistent treatment under the law. Tending to the computerized partition and advancing the far reaching reception of innovation in policing essential for a more comprehensive and compelling law enforcement framework.

Issues of Witness Security and Casualty Backing:

The security and prosperity of witnesses and casualties are principal in guaran-teeing the uprightness of the law enforcement process. In any case, witness security systems in India are frequently deficient, uncovering people who offer clues to ex-pected mischief or terrorizing. This absence of security can prevent observers from helping out policing, the possibilities of a fair preliminary.

Casualty support benefits likewise face difficulties regarding accessibility and openness. Numerous casualties, especially those from underestimated networks, may not know about their freedoms or the help administrations accessible to them. Reinforcing observer insurance gauges and upgrading casualty support adminis-trations are fundamental for cultivating a safer and steady climate inside the law enforcement framework.

Challenges in Scientific Science and Proof Taking care of:

The job of scientific science in criminal examinations is critical for laying out realities, recognizing culprits, and guaranteeing the respectability of proof. Be that as it may, challenges exist regarding the limit and capacities of legal research centers, the nature of scientific investigation, and the legitimate taking care of and conservation of proof.

Lacking assets and a build-up of cases in scientific research centers can prompt postpones in proof examination. Additionally, the absence of normalized conven-tions for proof assortment and capacity can think twice about suitability and unwa-vering quality of criminological proof in court. Reinforcing measurable capacities and laying out accepted procedures for proof taking care of are basic for upgrading the validity of the law enforcement framework.

1.2 Identifying key issues such as backlog of cases, outdated technology, and inadequate infrastructure

The Indian law enforcement framework, while being a foundation of keeping up with the rule of law, wrestles with a huge number of main points of interest that essentially influence its usefulness, effectiveness, and reasonableness. Three basic difficulties that stand apart are the determined build-up of cases, the commonness of obsolete innovation, and insufficient framework across different parts of the framework. Recognizing and resolving these main points of contention is basic for cultivating a more responsive, straightforward, and compelling law enforcement framework in India.

Overabundance of Cases:

One of the most major problems tormenting the Indian law enforcement framework is the significant overabundance of cases. The sheer volume of forthcoming cases, enveloping both common and criminal matters, represents a huge snag to the convenient conveyance of equity. The excess is especially articulated in lower courts, where the caseload frequently surpasses the limit with respect to speedy goal.

The results of this overabundance are broad. Drawn out defers in the removal of cases can prompt a forswearing of equity, influencing both the denounced and the people in question. For the denounced, expanded times of pre-preliminary confinement can bring about huge individual and financial difficulties, even before culpability is laid out. For casualties, postponed equity might dissolve trust in the overall set of laws and impede the conclusion and recuperating process.

A few variables add to the overabundance of cases. Inadequate legal framework, a lack of judges, procedural intricacies, and a sluggish paced lawful interaction all assume a part. Furthermore, the absence of elective question goal components and the ill-disposed nature of the general set of laws add to the amassing of cases in courts.

Tending to the overabundance of cases requires a multi-pronged methodology. Expanding the quantity of judges, particularly at the lower court levels, is a basic step. This requires enrollment as well as measures to hold experienced legal officials. Smoothing out strategies, advancing elective debate goal instruments, and utilizing innovation for case the board can add to the speedy removal of cases.

Obsolete Innovation:

The innovative scene inside the Indian law enforcement framework presents a critical test, portrayed by the predominance of obsolete innovation and a sluggish speed of mechanical reception. While mechanical progressions have changed different areas worldwide, the law enforcement framework in India frequently wrestles with out of date frameworks, manual cycles, and an absence of coordination.

Policing, specifically, face difficulties in embracing present day innovation for wrongdoing counteraction, examination, and proof administration. Obsolete data frameworks, deficient information stockpiling abilities, and restricted network ruin the opportune and successful trade of data among policing. This can block the quick goal of cases, compromise the nature of examinations, and impede the proactive ID of arising dangers.

With regards to the legal executive, obsolete innovation adds to the steadiness of manual record-keeping, lumbering case the board cycles, and restricted admittance to computerized court records. This dials back court procedures as well as hampers the productivity of legitimate examination and the dispersal of data to people in general.

To address the test of obsolete innovation, there is a requirement for critical interests in overhauling and modernizing the mechanical foundation of the law enforcement framework. This incorporates the execution of coordinated case the executives frameworks, computerized proof administration stages, and secure correspondence channels for policing. Preparing programs for policing, legal counselors, and legal officials are fundamental to guarantee powerful usage of present day innovation.

Deficient Framework:

Deficient framework is an unavoidable test across different parts of the law enforcement framework, enveloping police headquarters, courts, and restorative offices. The absence of legitimate framework hampers the proficient working of these foundations and adversely influences the nature of equity conveyed.

In police headquarters, deficient framework adds to squeezed working circumstances, restricted extra room, and lacking offices for prisoners. This not just trade offs the prosperity of police staff yet additionally hinders the legitimate dealing with and documentation of cases. Current police headquarters ought to be furnished with cutting edge offices, including measurable labs, computerized proof capacity, and devoted spaces for casualty/witness associations.

Court foundation, especially at the lower levels, faces difficulties, for example, deficient court space, obsolete offices, and a lack of care staff. This effects the limit of the legal executive to deal with cases effectively and adds to defers in court procedures. Updating court framework, assembling extra courts, and giving current conveniences can fundamentally work on the working of the legal framework.

Restorative offices, including detainment facilities, additionally wrestle with deficient framework. Stuffed penitentiaries, absence of appropriate sterilization, and restricted restoration offices add to a climate that isn't helpful for the renewal of detainees. Assembling new penitentiaries, modernizing existing offices, and integrating global guidelines for accommodating treatment are fundamental for guaranteeing the prosperity of detainees and working with their recovery.

Interconnected Nature of Difficulties:

It's vital to perceive that these major questions are interconnected, and tending to one frequently emphatically affects the others. For instance, utilizing present day innovation can add to the decrease of case overabundances by smoothing out case the executives processes, empowering electronic recording, and working with remote court procedures. Additionally, interests in satisfactory framework support the successful usage of innovation, guaranteeing that the advantages of modernization are understood.

Besides, these difficulties are implanted in more extensive fundamental issues, including administration, asset assignment, and strategy structures. An all encompassing and foundational approach is expected to achieve feasible upgrades in the law enforcement framework. This includes joint effort between different partners, including the legal executive, policing, legitimate experts, policymakers, and common society.

Strategy Changes and Administrative Changes:

Tending to the recognized difficulties requires complete strategy changes and regulative changes. The plan of a Public Prosecution Strategy that focuses on the goal of forthcoming cases, especially those including undertrials, is fundamental. Regulative changes ought to zero in on refreshing and modernizing criminal regulations, guaranteeing that they are in a state of harmony with contemporary cultural standards and address arising types of crime.

The reception of innovation driven strategies, for example, the digitization of court records, electronic case the executives, and internet documenting frameworks, can essentially add to decreasing case accumulations. Furthermore, strategies that advance the utilization of trend setting innovations in policing, as man-made reasoning for prescient policing and computerized criminology for examinations, can upgrade the productivity and adequacy of wrongdoing counteraction and goal.

Key asset portion is pivotal for defeating foundation challenges. Policymakers should focus on the advancement of current police headquarters, court buildings, and remedial offices. This includes monetary ventures as well as essential wanting to guarantee that the framework meets the advancing requirements of the law enforcement framework.

Limit Building and Preparing:

Limit building and preparing programs assume a critical part in tending to the difficulties inside the law enforcement framework. Preparing drives ought to be intended for judges, legal advisors, policing, and remedial staff to improve their comprehension and usage of current innovation. Specific preparation on case the executives, computerized proof taking care of, and arising patterns in wrongdoing can add to a more gifted and skilled labor force.

Moreover, preparing projects ought to zero in on sharpening law enforcement experts to issues of common liberties, variety, and orientation awareness. This is especially important with regards to observe security, casualty support, and the fair treatment of all people inside the law enforcement framework.

Local area Commitment and Lawful Education:

Drawing in with the local area and advancing lawful education are necessary parts of changing the law enforcement framework. Local area policing drives that cultivate positive connections between policing general society add to building trust and participation. Legitimate education programs, especially in country and minimized networks, can engage people to attest their privileges, partake in lawful cycles, and consider the law enforcement framework responsible.

Advancing elective debate goal components, like intercession and discretion, can likewise reduce the weight on the proper equity framework and add to opportune and practical goal of questions.

1.3 Impact of these challenges on the overall efficiency and fairness of the system

The distinguished difficulties inside the Indian law enforcement framework — to be specific, the diligent excess of cases, obsolete innovation, and deficient foundation — have expansive outcomes that fundamentally influence the general proficiency and decency of the framework. These difficulties interlace and make a complicated trap of issues that, whenever left ignored, can dissolve public trust, compromise the standards of equity, and obstruct the framework's capacity to successfully work.

Effect of Accumulation of Cases:

The excess of cases meaningfully affects the productivity and reasonableness of the Indian law enforcement framework. Deferred equity, originating from a mind-boggling caseload and slow legal cycles, straightforwardly subverts the established assurance of the right to a quick preliminary. The effect is felt across various aspects.

1. **Disavowal of Equity:** Delayed postpones on the off chance that goal deny equity to both the denounced and the people in question. People held in pre-preliminary confinement face delayed vulnerability and expected mischief to their own and monetary prosperity. Casualties, then again, may encounter dissatisfaction, tension, and a feeling of bad form because of the delayed judicial procedures.

2. **Disintegration of Public Trust:** The build-up adds to an impression of shortcoming and incapability in the law enforcement framework, dissolving public trust. At the point when residents see that the framework can't convey ideal equity, they might lose trust in the general set of laws' capacity to safe-guard their privileges and guarantee a fair and quick goal of debates.

3. **Trouble on the Overall set of laws:** The sheer volume of forthcoming cases puts a colossal weight on the general set of laws. Exhausted judges, investigators, and guard lawyers might battle to commit adequate time and

thoughtfulness regarding each case, possibly compromising the nature of judicial actions and the intensive assessment of proof.

4. **Influence on Undertrials:** The build-up excessively influences people anticipating preliminary. Numerous undertrials burn through broadened periods in confinement, at times longer than the possible sentence for the supposed offense. This abuses their right to freedom as well as lead to the deficiency of work, familial interruptions, and mental trouble.

Tending to the build-up of cases is, in this way, basic for reestablishing public confidence in the law enforcement framework, guaranteeing the convenient conveyance of equity, and maintaining the protected freedoms of people associated with legal procedures.

Effect of Obsolete Innovation:

The commonness of obsolete innovation inside the law enforcement framework obstructs its effectiveness and impedes the usage of present day instruments for wrongdoing anticipation, examination, and proof administration. The results of depending on out of date innovation resonate across different aspects of the framework.

1. **Wasteful Examinations:** Policing wrestle with obsolete data frameworks, preventing their capacity to productively gather, make due, and share critical data connected with crimes. Examinations might be compromised, and the opportune recognizable proof of arising dangers might be blocked.

2. **Defers in Judicial Procedures:** The utilization of manual cycles, obsolete record-keeping frameworks, and an absence of computerized court records add to postpones in legal procedures. This dials back court processes as well as limits admittance to convenient and exact data for lawful experts, obstructing their capacity to settle on informed choices.

3. **Compromised Proof Dealing with:** Obsolete innovation influences the appropriate taking care of and safeguarding of proof. Deficient advanced proof administration frameworks can prompt information debasement, misfortune, or control, compromising the honesty of proof introduced in court. This can affect the reasonableness of preliminaries and the unwavering quality of legal results.

4. **Restricted Admittance to Equity:** The advanced separation coming about because of obsolete innovation can make variations in admittance to equity. People without admittance to advanced assets might confront difficulties in documenting on the web protests, getting to legitimate data, or partaking in remote court procedures. This fuels existing financial abberations in the general set of laws.

Modernizing innovation inside the law enforcement framework is fundamental for upgrading its proficiency, straightforwardness, and adequacy. The reception of cutting edge devices for information investigation, advanced criminology, and get correspondence can essentially work on the framework's abilities and add to the fair organization of equity.

Effect of Deficient Framework:

Deficient framework across police headquarters, courts, and remedial offices significantly affects the general working of the law enforcement framework. The absence of legitimate offices and assets adds to fundamental shortcomings and compromises the prosperity of people inside the framework.

1. **Compromised Policing:** foundation in police headquarters can think twice about capacity of policing to actually do their obligations. Squeezed working circumstances, restricted extra room, and obsolete offices impede the legitimate documentation of cases, proof administration, and generally analytical cycles.

2. **Defers in Court Procedures:** Lacking court foundation, including a deficiency of courts and care staff, adds to postpones in court procedures. The absence of current conveniences, for example, video conferencing offices, can upset the productive direct of judicial actions, especially in the midst of emergency or crises.

3. **Challenges in Remedies:** Lacking framework in restorative offices, including stuffed penitentiaries and deficient recovery programs, presents difficulties to the transformation and restoration of prisoners.

   The absence of legitimate sterilization, medical services, and instructive offices inside jails adds to a climate that might block the fruitful reintegration of people into society upon discharge.

4. **Variations in Admittance to Equity:** Lacking framework compounds existing abberations in admittance to equity. People in provincial or under-estimated networks might confront extra difficulties in getting to police headquarters, courts, or remedial offices because of geological limitations or the shortfall of satisfactory transportation foundation.

Tending to framework challenges requires key preparation, asset portion, and a promise to making present day, exceptional offices across all parts of the law enforcement framework. Sufficient foundation isn't just essential for the effective working of the framework yet additionally for guaranteeing the prosperity of people inside the framework, including policing, legitimate experts, and those in care.

Interconnected Effect on In general Proficiency and Decency:

The interconnected idea of these difficulties makes a combined effect on the general proficiency and decency of the law enforcement framework. The accumulation of cases, obsolete innovation, and insufficient framework are not disconnected issues but instead intensify each other's ramifications.

1. **Aggregate Deferrals:** The build-up of cases, coming about because of a blend of procedural postponements and insufficient foundation, adds to combined defers across the whole law enforcement process. From the recording of a grievance to the goal of a case, delays at each stage obstruct the framework's general productivity.

2. **Disabled Nature of Equity:** Obsolete innovation compromises the nature of equity by blocking proficient examinations, proof administration, and court procedures. Insufficient foundation worsens these difficulties, establishing a climate where legitimate experts might battle to play out their obligations really, influencing the general decency of lawful results.

3. **Abberations in Access and Treatment:** Lacking foundation and obsolete innovation add to differences in admittance to equity, sustaining financial disparities. People without admittance to advanced assets or confronting geological requirements might encounter boundaries in exploring the general set of laws, prompting differences in the treatment they get.

4. **Burden on HR:** The combined effect of these difficulties overburdens HR inside the law enforcement framework. Exhausted judges, policing, and support staff might find it trying to keep up with elevated requirements of execution, prompting potential burnout, stress, and compromised independent direction.

The Requirement for Extensive Changes:

Tending to the effect of these difficulties requires extensive changes that focus on the main drivers and interdependencies inside the law enforcement framework. Strategy changes, regulative changes, limit building, and key asset distribution are fundamental parts of a comprehensive way to deal with rejuvenating the framework.

1. **Thorough Legitimate Changes:** Refreshing and modernizing lawful structures through complete official changes is an essential step. This incorporates tending to old fashioned regulations, smoothing out lawful methods, and integrating contemporary ways to deal with law enforcement. A Public Prosecution Strategy that focuses on the convenient goal of cases can essentially add to decreasing the excess.

2. **Mechanical Progressions:** Putting resources into current innovation and taking on cutting edge instruments for wrongdoing counteraction, examination, and case the board is pivotal. Executing coordinated data frameworks,

advanced proof administration stages, and secure correspondence channels can upgrade the proficiency and adequacy of the law enforcement framework.

3. **Vital Asset Designation:** Satisfactory asset distribution is fundamental for conquering framework challenges. This includes monetary speculations as well as essential intending to guarantee that police headquarters, courts, and restorative offices are furnished with present day offices, innovation, and thoroughly prepared work force.

4. **Limit Building and Preparing:** Preparing programs for judges, legal counselors, policing, and remedial staff are imperative for improving their comprehension and use of present day innovation. Specific preparation on case the board, computerized proof dealing with, and arising patterns in wrong-doing can add to a more gifted and skilled labor force.

5. **Local area Commitment and Lawful Education:** Drawing in with the local area and advancing legitimate proficiency are essential parts of change. Local area policing drives, legitimate mindfulness projects, and advancement of elective question goal components can cultivate positive cooperations between the law enforcement framework and the general population.

6. **Global Accepted procedures:** Gaining from worldwide accepted procedures and benchmarks can give important bits of knowledge to changing the law enforcement framework. Joint effort with global associations, sharing of information, and taking on fruitful models from different purviews can speed up the speed of changes.

Chapter 2

Lok Sabha's Vision for Reform

The Lok Sabha, as the lower place of India's Parliament, assumes an essential part in molding the regulative scene of the country. Lately, the Lok Sabha has shown a guarantee to tending to the complex difficulties inside the law enforcement framework and cultivating significant changes. The vision for change envelops regulative changes, strategy drives, and a cooperative methodology with different parts of government, common society, and people in general. This thorough vision mirrors an acknowledgment of the developing necessities of Indian culture and the basic to fabricate a law enforcement framework that is effective, fair, and receptive to the different requirements of its residents.

Authoritative Changes:

A focal part of the Lok Sabha's vision for transforming the law enforcement framework includes regulative changes that line up with contemporary cultural standards and address arising difficulties. The course of legitimate change requires a nuanced comprehension of the intricacies inside the framework, and the Lok Sabha has shown a guarantee to establishing regulations that are moderate, only, and as one with the standards cherished in the Constitution.

1. **Modernization of Criminal Regulations:** The Lok Sabha perceives the basic to modernize criminal regulations to guarantee their significance in the current setting. This incorporates a survey and revision of old rules that may not satisfactorily address contemporary types of crime. The accentuation is on guaranteeing that the legitimate structure is dynamic, responsive, and fit for tending to arising difficulties in wrongdoing and equity.

2. **Public Prosecution Strategy:** As a component of its vision for speedy goal of cases, the Lok Sabha has been instrumental in figuring out and carrying out a Public Suit Strategy. This strategy focuses on the ideal removal of cases,

especially zeroing in on diminishing the excess that troubles the legal framework. By advancing elective debate goal instruments and smoothing out legitimate cycles, the arrangement expects to improve the proficiency of the law enforcement framework.

3. **Regulative Shields for Weak Populaces:** The Lok Sabha recognizes the requirement for official shields to safeguard weak populaces inside the law enforcement framework. This incorporates ordering regulations and arrangements that address issues like separation, savagery against minimized networks, and the privileges of ladies and youngsters. By focusing on the institution of regulations that safeguard the privileges of weak populaces, the Lok Sabha tries to encourage a more comprehensive and simply lawful structure.

Advancement of Innovation and Development:

The Lok Sabha's vision for improving the law enforcement framework perceives the groundbreaking capability of innovation and development. Utilizing present day innovation is viewed as a vital technique to upgrade the proficiency, straightforwardness, and viability of different parts inside the framework, from policing court procedures and revisions.

1. **Digitalization of Legitimate Cycles:** The Lok Sabha upholds the digitalization of lawful cycles to smooth out case the board, work with internet documenting, and guarantee the availability of court records. This incorporates the reception of coordinated data frameworks that empower consistent joint effort among various partners inside the law enforcement framework.

2. **Headways in Scientific Science:** Perceiving the vital job of measurable science in criminal examinations, the Lok Sabha advocates for progressions in criminological advancements. This includes putting resources into best in class scientific labs, advancing innovative work in criminological science, and laying out normalized conventions for proof assortment and examination.

3. **Network safety Measures:** because of the advancing idea of wrongdoing, especially in the computerized domain, the Lok Sabha focuses on network protection measures. This incorporates regulative drives to address cybercrime, improve the capacities of policing in managing advanced proof, and lay out strong components for shielding the nation's network protection.

Framework Advancement:

The Lok Sabha's vision for change stretches out to tending to the framework challenges looked by different parts of the law enforcement framework. Satisfactory framework is considered basic for the productive working of police headquarters, courts, and restorative offices.

1. **Modernization of Police headquarters:** Perceiving the significance of policing keeping public control, the Lok Sabha upholds drives for the modernization of police headquarters. This includes giving current offices, overhauling innovation and hardware, and guaranteeing a helpful work space for police staff.

2. **Court Offices and Innovation:** The Lok Sabha advocates for the improvement of court offices and the mix of innovation to upgrade the effectiveness of court procedures. This incorporates the foundation of exceptional court edifices, video conferencing offices for distant hearings, and the digitization of court records to work with simpler access and recovery.

3. **Restorative Office Redesigns:** The Lok Sabha focuses on the improvement of remedial offices, including jails, with an emphasis on decongestion, sterilization, and recovery. Satisfactory framework inside remedial offices is viewed as fundamental for establishing a climate that advances the renewal and reintegration of people into society.

Limit Building and Preparing:

Perceiving the significance of HR inside the law enforcement framework, the Lok Sabha underscores limit building and preparing programs. These drives are intended to improve the abilities, information, and incredible skill of judges, attorneys, policing, and restorative staff.

1. **Legal Preparation Projects:** The Lok Sabha upholds thorough preparation programs for judges to upgrade how they might interpret present day lawful standards, arising difficulties, and progressions in legitimate innovation. This incorporates progressing proficient improvement to guarantee that judges are exceptional to explore complex lawful issues.

2. **Policing Drives:** Preparing drives for policing are a vital part of the Lok Sabha's vision. These projects intend to work on insightful methods, elevate adherence to common liberties principles, and improve the utilization of current innovation for viable wrongdoing anticipation and goal.

3. **Legitimate Schooling Changes:** The Lok Sabha perceives the significance of lawful training in molding the up and coming age of legitimate experts. Changes in legitimate schooling, including educational plan refreshes, mix of innovation in legitimate examinations, and accentuation on reasonable abilities, are focused on to guarantee that attorneys are good to go for the advancing lawful scene.

Local area Commitment and Legitimate Education:

The Lok Sabha imagines a law enforcement framework that isn't simply receptive to legitimate experts yet in addition effectively draws in with the local area. Drives advancing lawful education, local area policing, and elective question goal instruments are essential to cultivating a more comprehensive and participatory overall set of laws.

1. **Lawful Education Missions:** The Lok Sabha upholds far reaching legitimate proficiency crusades pointed toward engaging residents to figure out their privileges, access legitimate assets, and effectively partake in the lawful cycle. This includes outreach programs, instructive drives, and the spread of legitimate data in open configurations.

2. **Local area Policing Drives:** Perceiving the significance of building trust between policing and the local area, the Lok Sabha advances local area policing drives. These projects mean to fortify the connection between the police and the general population, improve participation, and address neighborhood concerns cooperatively.

3. **Elective Question Goal Instruments:** The Lok Sabha supports the advancement of elective debate goal components, like intervention and discretion, to lighten the weight on the conventional equity framework. This includes making mindfulness about elective strategies for debate goal and laying out components to work with their execution.

Global Coordinated effort and Best Practices:

In quest for its vision for change, the Lok Sabha perceives the worth of global joint effort and gaining from best practices around the world. Drawing in with worldwide associations, looking for aptitude from different wards, and embracing effective models are essential to the Lok Sabha's way to deal with improvement in law enforcement.

1. **Cooperation with Worldwide Associations:** The Lok Sabha effectively draws in with worldwide associations, like the Assembled Countries, to team up on drives connected with common liberties, lawful changes, and the headway of worldwide principles in law enforcement. This includes partaking in meetings, sharing encounters, and adding to worldwide endeavors in the field.

2. **Gaining from Best Practices:** The Lok Sabha tries to gain from and embrace best practices saw in different nations with fruitful law enforcement frameworks. This incorporates concentrating on imaginative methodologies, official structures, and mechanical arrangements that have exhibited positive results in tending to comparable difficulties.

2.1 Overview of Lok Sabha's commitment to modernizing the criminal justice system

The Lok Sabha, as the lower place of the Indian Parliament, has shown an immovable obligation to modernizing the law enforcement framework, perceiving the basic for changes that line up with contemporary cultural necessities. The complex idea of this responsibility envelops administrative drives, strategy structures, mechanical headways, foundation improvement, limit building, local area commitment, and global coordinated effort. This extensive methodology mirrors the Lok Sabha's commitment to making a law enforcement framework that is productive, fair, straightforward, and receptive to the developing difficulties looked by the country.

Official Drives:

One of the essential articulations of the Lok Sabha's obligation to modernization is clear in its authoritative drives pointed toward achieving considerable changes in the lawful structure administering the law enforcement framework. The Lok Sabha perceives the requirement for regulations that are in accordance with sacred standards as well as receptive to the changing idea of wrongdoing and cultural assumptions.

1. **Modernizing Criminal Regulations:** The Lok Sabha has been at the very front of endeavors to modernize India's criminal regulations. This includes an exhaustive survey and correction of existing rules to guarantee their significance and viability in tending to contemporary types of crime. The goal is to make a legitimate system that is versatile, proportionate, and equipped for tending to arising difficulties while maintaining the standards of equity and common liberties.

2. **Public Case Strategy:** Fundamental to the Lok Sabha's responsibility is the detailing and execution of a Public Prosecution Strategy. This strategy focuses on the opportune goal of cases, with a particular spotlight on decreasing the build-up that has tormented the legal framework. By empowering elective question goal instruments and smoothing out lawful cycles, the Public Case Strategy plans to improve the productivity of the law enforcement framework.

3. **Administrative Shields for Weak Populaces:** Perceiving the weaknesses looked by specific portions of society, the Lok Sabha has done whatever it takes to order regulation that gives protections to these populaces. This incorporates regulations tending to separation, brutality against underestimated networks, and upgraded assurance for the privileges of ladies and youngsters inside the law enforcement framework.

Advancement of Innovation and Development:

Embracing innovative headways is a critical mainstay of the Lok Sabha's obligation to modernizing the law enforcement framework. The Lok Sabha recognizes the groundbreaking capability of innovation in upgrading the proficiency, straightforwardness, and viability of different parts inside the framework.

1. **Digitalization of Lawful Cycles:** The Lok Sabha effectively upholds the digitalization of legitimate cycles to smooth out case the executives, work with web based documenting, and guarantee the availability of court records. This incorporates the reception of coordinated data frameworks that empower consistent joint effort among various partners inside the law enforcement framework.

2. **Progressions in Scientific Science:** Perceiving the crucial job of measurable science in criminal examinations, the Lok Sabha advocates for headways in criminological advancements. This includes huge interests in best in class measurable labs, innovative work in scientific science, and the foundation of normalized conventions for proof assortment and examination.

3. **Network protection Measures:** With a comprehension of the developing dangers in the advanced domain, the Lok Sabha stresses the significance of network safety measures. This incorporates regulative drives to address cybercrime, upgrade the capacities of policing in managing computerized proof, and lay out hearty components for defending the nation's online protection.

Foundation Advancement:

A basic part of the Lok Sabha's obligation to modernization is tending to the foundation challenges looked by different parts of the law enforcement framework. Satisfactory framework is viewed as basic for the proficient working of police headquarters, courts, and remedial offices.

1. **Modernization of Police headquarters:** Perceiving the essential job of policing keeping public control, the Lok Sabha advocates for the modernization of police headquarters. This includes giving present day offices, overhauling innovation and hardware, and guaranteeing a helpful work space for police staff.

2. **Court Offices and Innovation:** The Lok Sabha focuses on the improvement of court offices and the joining of innovation to upgrade the proficiency of court procedures. This incorporates the foundation of exceptional court buildings, video conferencing offices for far off hearings, and the digitization of court records to work with more straightforward access and recovery.

3. **Remedial Office Overhauls:** Recognizing the significance of restorative offices in the recovery of wrongdoers, the Lok Sabha highlights the requirement for development in foundation inside jails. This includes resolving

issues, for example, congestion, disinfection, and the arrangement of restoration projects to establish a climate helpful for reconstruction.

Limit Building and Preparing:

Perceiving the basic job of HR inside the law enforcement framework, the Lok Sabha underscores limit building and preparing programs. These drives are intended to upgrade the abilities, information, and incredible skill of judges, legal advisors, policing, and restorative staff.

1. **Legal Preparation Projects:** The Lok Sabha effectively upholds complete preparation programs for judges to improve how they might interpret present day legitimate standards, arising difficulties, and headways in lawful innovation. This incorporates continuous expert advancement to guarantee that judges are exceptional to explore complex lawful issues.

2. **Policing Drives:** Preparing drives for policing are a focal part of the Lok Sabha's vision. These projects mean to work on insightful methods, elevate adherence to common freedoms guidelines, and improve the utilization of present day innovation for viable wrongdoing avoidance and goal.

3. **Legitimate Schooling Changes:** Perceiving the significance of lawful training in molding the up and coming age of legitimate experts, the Lok Sabha advocates for changes in legitimate instruction. This incorporates updates to the educational plan, joining of innovation in legitimate examinations, and an accentuation on pragmatic abilities to guarantee that attorneys are completely ready for the advancing lawful scene.

Local area Commitment and Legitimate Proficiency:

A striking part of the Lok Sabha's obligation to modernizing the law enforcement framework is its emphasis on local area commitment and legitimate proficiency. Drives advancing lawful mindfulness, local area policing, and elective question goal components are basic to encouraging a more comprehensive and participatory overall set of laws.

1. **Legitimate Proficiency Missions:** The Lok Sabha effectively advances lawful education crusades pointed toward engaging residents to grasp their privileges, access legitimate assets, and effectively partake in the lawful cycle. This includes outreach programs, instructive drives, and the scattering of lawful data in open organizations.

2. **Local area Policing Drives:** Perceiving the significance of building trust between policing and the local area, the Lok Sabha upholds local area policing drives. These projects intend to reinforce the connection between the police

and people in general, upgrade participation, and address nearby worries cooperatively.

3. **Elective Debate Goal Instruments:** The Lok Sabha energizes the advancement of elective question goal components, like intercession and assertion, to lighten the weight on the conventional equity framework. This includes making mindfulness about elective techniques for question goal and laying out components to work with their execution.

Worldwide Cooperation and Best Practices:

In accordance with its obligation to modernization, the Lok Sabha puts major areas of strength for an on global cooperation and gaining from best practices around the world. Drawing in with global associations, looking for skill from different locales, and embracing fruitful models are vital to the Lok Sabha's way to deal with enhancement in law enforcement.

1. **Coordinated effort with Worldwide Associations:** The Lok Sabha effectively draws in with worldwide associations, like the Unified Countries, to team up on drives connected with basic liberties, legitimate changes, and the headway of worldwide norms in law enforcement. This includes taking part in meetings, sharing encounters, and adding to worldwide endeavors in the field.

2. **Gaining from Best Practices:** The Lok Sabha looks to gain from and take on accepted procedures saw in different nations with effective law enforcement frameworks. This incorporates concentrating on creative methodologies, official systems, and mechanical arrangements that have shown positive results in tending to comparable difficulties.

2.2 Presentation of key initiatives and policy frameworks proposed by Lok Sabha

The Lok Sabha, India's lower place of Parliament, has been at the very front of proposing key drives and strategy structures to address the mind boggling difficulties inside the country's law enforcement framework. These drives mirror an exhaustive way to deal with modernize and change the framework, including regulative changes, innovative headways, foundation improvement, limit building, local area commitment, and worldwide joint effort. The Lok Sabha's obligation to these drives highlights its acknowledgment of the requirement for a responsive, proficient, and fair law enforcement framework that lines up with sacred standards and meets the developing necessities of Indian culture.

1. **Authoritative Changes:**

A foundation of the Lok Sabha's plan for modernizing the law enforcement framework includes critical regulative changes. These changes are pointed toward refreshing and adjusting existing regulations to contemporary difficulties and cultural assumptions.

Modernization of Criminal Regulations: The Lok Sabha has been effectively participated during the time spent modernizing criminal regulations. This drive includes an exhaustive survey of obsolete resolutions and the acquaintance of changes with guarantee that the legitimate structure is in a state of harmony with the current socio-lawful scene. The goal is to address arising types of crime, eliminate old fashioned arrangements, and make a general set of laws that is receptive to developing cultural standards.

Public Prosecution Strategy: The detailing and execution of a Public Suit Strategy is a urgent regulative drive by the Lok Sabha. This strategy focuses on the ideal goal of cases, with an emphasis on lessening the build-up that has long tormented the Indian legal framework. By advancing elective debate goal components and smoothing out lawful cycles, the approach plans to improve the proficiency of the law enforcement framework and assist the goal of cases.

Administrative Shields for Weak Populaces: Perceiving the weaknesses looked by specific fragments of society, the Lok Sabha has presented regulation pointed toward giving improved shields. This incorporates regulations tending to segregation, viciousness against underestimated networks, and explicit insurances for the privileges of ladies and kids inside the law enforcement framework. These official measures mirror a pledge to encouraging inclusivity and insurance for weak populaces.

2. **Advancement of Innovation and Development:**

The Lok Sabha recognizes the extraordinary capability of innovation in reshaping the law enforcement scene. Through different drives, it looks to bridle mechanical headways to upgrade the effectiveness and straightforwardness of the framework.

Digitalization of Lawful Cycles: Embracing the computerized age, the Lok Sabha effectively upholds the digitalization of legitimate cycles. This drive means to smooth out case the board, work with web based documenting, and guarantee the openness of court records. Coordinated data frameworks are being acquainted with empower consistent joint effort among various partners inside the law enforcement framework.

Headways in Scientific Science: Perceiving the basic job of measurable science in criminal examinations, the Lok Sabha advocates for progressions in criminological advancements. This includes significant interests in best in class scientific labs, innovative work in measurable science, and the foundation of normalized conventions for proof assortment and examination. The objective is to use state of the art innovation to reinforce the analytical cycles.

Online protection Measures: in light of the rising difficulties presented by cybercrime, the Lok Sabha stresses the significance of network safety measures. Administrative drives are being acquainted with address digital dangers, upgrade the capacities of policing in managing computerized proof, and lay out strong components for protecting the nation's network safety. This perceives the need to remain in front of mechanical headways took advantage of by crooks.

3. **Foundation Improvement:**

An essential part of the Lok Sabha's modernization plan is the improvement of framework inside the law enforcement framework. Satisfactory framework is seen as fundamental for the smooth working of police headquarters, courts, and restorative offices.

Modernization of Police headquarters: Perceiving the focal job of policing keeping public control, the Lok Sabha advocates for the modernization of police headquarters. This drive includes giving current offices, redesigning innovation and hardware, and guaranteeing a helpful workplace for police faculty. The point is to upgrade the proficiency and viability of policing.

Court Offices and Innovation: The Lok Sabha focuses on the advancement of court offices and the mix of innovation to upgrade the productivity of court procedures. This incorporates the foundation of exceptional court edifices, video conferencing offices for far off hearings, and the digitization of court records to work with more straightforward access and recovery. Further developed foundation inside courts is viewed as basic for speeding up lawful cycles.

Restorative Office Updates: Recognizing the significance of remedial offices in the recovery of wrongdoers, the Lok Sabha underscores the requirement for development in foundation inside penitentiaries. This includes resolving issues, for example, congestion, sterilization, and the arrangement of recovery projects to establish a climate helpful for reconstruction. Updated framework is viewed as imperative for the fruitful reintegration of people into society.

4. **Limit Building and Preparing:**

The Lok Sabha perceives the critical job of HR inside the law enforcement framework and puts major areas of strength for an on limit building and preparing programs.

Legal Preparation Projects: The Lok Sabha effectively upholds complete preparation programs for judges to improve how they might interpret present day legitimate standards, arising difficulties, and headways in lawful innovation. This incorporates continuous expert improvement to guarantee that judges are exceptional to explore complex lawful issues and convey equity really.

Policing Drives: Preparing drives for policing structure a focal part of the Lok Sabha's vision. These projects mean to work on analytical procedures, elevate adherence to basic freedoms norms, and upgrade the utilization of present day innovation for powerful wrongdoing anticipation and goal. Thoroughly prepared policing are seen as fundamental for maintaining law and order.

Legitimate Schooling Changes: Perceiving the significance of lawful training in molding the up and coming age of legitimate experts, the Lok Sabha advocates for changes in legitimate instruction. This incorporates updates to the educational plan, joining of innovation in legitimate examinations, and an accentuation on reasonable abilities to guarantee that attorneys are good to go for the developing lawful scene. A changed legitimate schooling system is viewed as crucial for delivering skilled and moral lawful experts.

5. **Local area Commitment and Lawful Proficiency:**

   Local area commitment and the advancement of lawful proficiency are vital parts of the Lok Sabha's modernization plan. These drives plan to engage residents, upgrade trust in the law enforcement framework, and give elective roads to debate goal.

   Lawful Proficiency Missions: The Lok Sabha effectively advances legitimate education crusades pointed toward enabling residents to grasp their freedoms, access legitimate assets, and effectively partake in the lawful cycle. This includes outreach programs, instructive drives, and the dispersal of lawful data in available organizations. Legitimate education is viewed as a way to fortify the's comprehension public might interpret the general set of laws.

   Local area Policing Drives: Perceiving the significance of building trust between policing and the local area, the Lok Sabha upholds local area policing drives. These projects mean to reinforce the connection between the police and general society, improve participation, and address nearby worries co-operatively. Local area policing is seen as a proactive way to deal with keeping public control.

   Elective Debate Goal Components: The Lok Sabha energizes the advancement of elective question goal instruments, like intercession and discretion, to ease the weight on the conventional equity framework. This includes making mindfulness about elective strategies for question goal and laying out components to work with their execution. Elective question goal is viewed as a method for giving faster and more open equity.

6. **Global Cooperation and Best Practices:**

In its quest for modernizing the law enforcement framework, the Lok Sabha accentuates the significance of global coordinated effort and gaining from best practices around the world.

Joint effort with Worldwide Associations: The Lok Sabha effectively draws in with global associations, like the Assembled Countries, to team up on drives connected with common freedoms, lawful changes, and the headway of worldwide guidelines in law enforcement. This includes taking part in meetings, sharing encounters, and adding to global endeavors in the field. Worldwide joint effort is viewed as a road for acquiring experiences and embracing worldwide accepted procedures.

Gaining from Best Practices: The Lok Sabha looks to gain from and embrace best practices saw in different nations with fruitful law enforcement frameworks. This incorporates concentrating on imaginative methodologies, authoritative systems, and mechanical arrangements that have shown positive results in tending to comparative difficulties. Gaining from worldwide prescribed procedures is seen as an essential way to deal with illuminate and improve homegrown change endeavors.

2.3 Explanation of the rationale behind these initiatives

The drives proposed by the Lok Sabha for the modernization of the law enforcement framework in India are driven by a smart and complex reasoning. The difficulties looked by the current framework, including obsolete regulations, innovative holes, foundation lacks, and issues connected with limit and local area commitment, have required a far reaching and ground breaking approach. The Lok Sabha's drives are grounded in the standards of equity, effectiveness, reasonableness, and responsiveness to the advancing requirements of Indian culture.

1. **Administrative Changes:**

   The reasoning behind the administrative changes started by the Lok Sabha lies in the affirmation of the advancing idea of wrongdoing and the basic to guarantee that the lawful structure stays pertinent and compelling. The modernization of criminal regulations is driven by the need to address contemporary types of crime, wipe out old arrangements, and make a general set of laws that lines up with protected standards and cultural standards.

   The Public Prosecution Strategy is supported by the comprehension that the excess of cases represents a critical test to the law enforcement framework. The arrangement means to facilitate case goal by focusing on elective question goal components and smoothing out lawful cycles. This is established in the acknowledgment that a quick and productive lawful cycle is urgent for maintaining the right to a rapid preliminary and guaranteeing admittance to equity for all.

   Regulative shields for weak populaces are inspired by the obligation to safeguard the freedoms of underestimated networks, ladies, and youngsters inside the law enforcement framework. This mirrors an acknowledgment of verifiable treacheries and an assurance to make a lawful structure that is comprehensive, evenhanded, and delicate to the novel difficulties looked by these populaces.

2. **Advancement of Innovation and Development:**

The accentuation on innovation and development in the Lok Sabha's drives is driven by the comprehension that modernizing the law enforcement framework requires utilizing progressions to upgrade proficiency, straightforwardness, and adequacy.

The digitalization of legitimate cycles is inspired by a craving to smooth out case the executives, diminish desk work, and make judicial procedures more open. By embracing coordinated data frameworks, the Lok Sabha means to make a cooperative and interconnected legitimate environment that works with effective correspondence and data dividing between various partners in the law enforcement framework.

Headways in criminological science and network protection measures are reactions to the changing idea of wrongdoing, especially in the advanced domain. The Lok Sabha perceives that putting resources into state of the art scientific advancements and network safety measures is fundamental for remaining in front of lawbreakers who exploit mechanical weaknesses. This approach mirrors a guarantee to guaranteeing that the law enforcement framework is prepared to deal with arising difficulties and really explore and indict cybercrimes.

3. **Foundation Improvement:**

The emphasis on foundation improvement inside the law enforcement framework is established in the comprehension that the physical and mechanical climate in which equity is regulated assumes a significant part in its productivity and openness.

The modernization of police headquarters is driven by the acknowledgment that policing are at the cutting edge of keeping public control. Redesigning police headquarters offices, giving present day hardware, and establishing a favorable workplace for police staff are fundamental stages to improve their viability in forestalling and researching wrongdoing.

Court offices and innovation updates are propelled by the need to address difficulties in the legal cycle. Exceptional court buildings, video conferencing offices, and digitized court records are viewed as essential parts for speeding up judicial procedures, diminishing deferrals, and guaranteeing that equity is controlled as soon a possible.

Remedial office updates are grounded in the comprehension that jails assume a crucial part in the recovery and transformation of wrongdoers. Further developing foundation inside restorative offices resolves issues of congestion, sterilization, and the arrangement of recovery programs, establishing a climate that upholds the fruitful reintegration of people into society.

4. **Limit Building and Preparing:**

The accentuation on limit building and preparing programs is spurred by the acknowledgment that HR are the foundation of the law enforcement framework. Thoroughly prepared and gifted staff are fundamental for the powerful working of the framework.

Legal preparation programs are intended to guarantee that judges are outfitted with the information and abilities important to explore complex lawful issues. Ceaseless expert improvement is viewed as critical for keeping up with the trustworthiness and skill of the legal executive, cultivating a more profound comprehension of arising lawful standards, and advancing consistency in direction.

Policing drives expect to upgrade the capacities of police faculty in analytical strategies, adherence to common liberties principles, and the utilization of current innovation. This perceives that a thoroughly prepared and proficient policing is fundamental for maintaining law and order and safeguarding the privileges of residents.

Legitimate training changes are persuaded by the comprehension that the lawful calling assumes a focal part in the organization of equity. Changes in legitimate training, including updates to the educational plan and the coordination of innovation, guarantee that future attorneys are good to go to explore the intricacies of the lawful scene and contribute actually to the equity framework.

5. **Local area Commitment and Lawful Education:**

The emphasis on local area commitment and lawful proficiency is established in the acknowledgment that a very much educated and drew out in the open is fundamental for the progress of the law enforcement framework.

Legitimate education crusades are propelled by the conviction that an educated populace is better prepared to figure out their freedoms, access lawful assets, and effectively take part in the legitimate cycle. By advancing legitimate education, the Lok Sabha means to enable residents to explore the overall set of laws and add to the organization of equity.

Local area policing drives are driven by the comprehension that building trust between policing and the local area is fundamental for compelling wrongdoing anticipation and goal. Drawing in with the local area, tending to neighborhood concerns, and cultivating participation add to a more cooperative and steady connection between the police and general society.

Advancement of elective question goal components mirrors a pledge to giving residents open and ideal roads for settling debates. By making mindfulness about elective techniques for debate goal, the Lok Sabha means to mitigate the weight on the conventional equity framework and advance a more effective and responsive way to deal with compromise.

6. Worldwide Coordinated effort and Best Practices:

The accentuation on worldwide coordinated effort and gaining from best practices is established in the acknowledgment that the difficulties inside the Indian law enforcement framework are not exceptional and that bits of knowledge from worldwide encounters can illuminate viable changes.

Coordinated effort with worldwide associations mirrors a pledge to adjusting India's law enforcement situation to worldwide common freedoms norms and best practices. By effectively taking part in worldwide drives, the Lok Sabha means to add to the worldwide talk on lawful changes and advantage from shared encounters.

Gaining from best practices saw in different nations is driven by the conviction that effective models can illuminate and speed up changes in India. Concentrating on creative methodologies, administrative systems, and innovative arrangements from around the world permits the Lok Sabha to adjust demonstrated techniques to the Indian setting.

Chapter 3

Legislative Reforms

Regulative changes stand as a foundation of the Lok Sabha's complex way to deal with modernizing the law enforcement framework in India. Perceiving the developing idea of wrongdoing, cultural assumptions, and the requirement for a legitimate structure that is responsive, effective, and just, the Lok Sabha has been proactive in starting changes across different elements of criminal regulations. These regulative endeavors are driven by a complete comprehension of the difficulties inside the current lawful structure and a guarantee to adjusting it to established standards, contemporary standards, and the changing scene of crimes.

1. **Modernization of Criminal Regulations:**

   The Lok Sabha's obligation to modernizing criminal regulations mirrors a consciousness of the obsolete and old nature of specific resolutions that may not satisfactorily address contemporary types of crime. This drive tries to exhaustively survey and alter existing regulations to guarantee their importance and adequacy in tending to developing difficulties.

   The reasoning behind modernization lies in the basic to connect holes in the legitimate structure and prepare it to battle new and complex types of criminal way of behaving actually. Obsolete regulations thwart the quest for equity as well as lead to potential premature deliveries where legitimate arrangements neglect to catch the subtleties of present day wrongdoing.

   By refreshing these regulations, the Lok Sabha expects to guarantee that the general set of laws stays a strong and versatile device for tending to the different scope of crimes pervasive in the public eye.

   In addition, modernization lines up with sacred standards, advancing the security of key freedoms and guaranteeing that legitimate arrangements are together as one with the developing principles of equity. The Lok Sabha's obligation to this regulative change mirrors an acknowledgment of the powerful idea of society and the basic to have a legitimate structure that can successfully answer arising difficulties while maintaining the standards of equity and common liberties.

2. **Public Prosecution Strategy:**

The plan and execution of a Public Suit Strategy address an essential drive by the Lok Sabha to resolve the enduring issue of case build-up inside the legal framework. The reasoning behind this strategy is established in the comprehension that postponed equity not just sabotages public trust in the general set of laws yet in addition disregards the protected right to a rapid preliminary.

The approach focuses on the ideal goal of cases through different means, including elective debate goal instruments. The accentuation on elective question goal lines up with the more extensive vision of decreasing the weight on conventional court processes and facilitating the goal of debates. By empowering gatherings to investigate elective roads for settling their debates, the strategy plans to ease the stress on the overburdened legal framework.

The reasoning additionally reaches out to the more extensive objectives of legal proficiency and asset streamlining. A decrease in the excess of cases guarantees a fair outcome is given expeditiously as well as permits the legal executive to zero in on additional complicated issues that require exhaustive consultation. This regulative change, subsequently, mirrors a promise to upgrading the proficiency and viability of the law enforcement framework, adding to the more extensive objectives of legal change and admittance to equity.

3. **Authoritative Shields for Weak Populaces:**

The Lok Sabha's obligation to sanctioning regulative protections for weak populaces inside the law enforcement framework is established in a profound comprehension of the verifiable and fundamental difficulties looked by these gatherings. This incorporates minimized networks, ladies, and kids, who frequently experience interesting weaknesses inside the lawful interaction.

The reasoning behind these official drives is to address authentic treacheries, separation, and viciousness looked by weak populaces. By authorizing explicit regulations, the Lok Sabha intends to give upgraded lawful assurance, perceive the exceptional difficulties looked by these gatherings, and advance inclusivity inside the law enforcement framework.

For example, regulations tending to separation and brutality against underestimated networks are driven by the acknowledgment that specific gatherings have generally been exposed to foundational inclinations and biases. Official changes in this setting mean to amend these authentic wrongs, advance equity under the steady gaze of the law, and guarantee that people from minimized networks get fair and unprejudiced treatment inside the law enforcement framework.

Also, authoritative shields for ladies and youngsters perceive the requirement for exceptional insurances attributable to their weak status. The Lok Sabha's obligation to these shields is grounded in the comprehension that the overall set of laws should be prepared to address the extraordinary difficulties looked by ladies and youngsters, giving them roads for assurance, recovery, and redressal.

4. **Complete Audit and Correction:**

The Lok Sabha's obligation to a complete survey and revision of criminal regulations means a proactive way to deal with guarantee that administrative arrangements stay significant and powerful. This drive is directed by an acknowledgment that the legitimate system should develop in light of cultural changes, arising difficulties, and progressions in lawful standards.

The reasoning behind this drive is to direct an intensive assessment of existing regulations, distinguish holes, and address ambiguities that might hinder the effective organization of equity. By embraced a far reaching survey, the Lok Sabha intends to make a lawful structure that is clear, sound, and fit for answering the different necessities of society.

This official change is likewise determined by a pledge to adjust the lawful system to established standards and worldwide basic freedoms principles. A far reaching survey takes into consideration the ID and correction of arrangements that might be conflicting with key privileges or neglect to fulfill contemporary guidelines of equity. The Lok Sabha's obligation to this interaction mirrors a commitment to maintaining law and order and guaranteeing that the overall set of laws stays a vigorous underwriter of equity for all.

5. **Regulative Protections for Casualties:**

One more basic part of the Lok Sabha's administrative changes is the presentation of shields for casualties inside the law enforcement framework. This drive is grounded in the acknowledgment that casualties frequently face difficulties during official procedures, including issues connected with security, backing, and pay.

The reasoning behind these regulative protections is to give a more casualty driven approach inside the lawful system. By sanctioning regulations that focus on the freedoms and prosperity of casualties, the Lok Sabha intends to address the power awkwardness that frequently exists among casualties and charged people inside the law enforcement process.

These shields might incorporate arrangements for witness security, pay for casualties, and instruments to guarantee that casualties are treated with pride and regard all through legal actions. By integrating these shields into the legitimate structure, the Lok Sabha tries to make a more adjusted and others conscious law enforcement framework that considers the privileges and needs of casualties.

6. **Accentuation on Helpful Equity:**

The Lok Sabha's regulative changes likewise stress supportive equity standards, flagging a takeoff from conventional correctional methodologies toward a more rehabilitative and local area situated model. The reasoning behind this shift is established in the comprehension that tending to the underlying drivers of criminal way of behaving and elevating restoration can add to long haul cultural prosperity.

Supportive equity centers around fixing the damage brought about by criminal way of behaving and includes dynamic investment by all partners, including wrong-doers, casualties, and the local area. The Lok Sabha's obligation to integrating supportive equity standards into the legitimate structure is driven by the conviction that this approach can prompt improved results concerning recovery, decreased recidivism, and local area recuperating.

By establishing regulations that advance helpful equity, the Lok Sabha means to encourage a more comprehensive and comprehensive law enforcement framework. This incorporates systems for elective question goal, casualty wrongdoer intercession, and local area based mediations. The reasoning behind these drives is to move past correctional measures and investigate approaches that address the hidden reasons for criminal way of behaving while at the same time including the impacted gatherings in the goal cycle.

3.1 Examination of key legislative changes proposed or enacted by Lok Sabha

The Lok Sabha, India's lower place of Parliament, has been instrumental in proposing and ordering key administrative changes pointed toward modernizing the law enforcement framework. These changes, mirroring a complete and ground breaking approach, address different features of the legitimate structure, going from the modernization of criminal regulations to the presentation of casualty driven changes and the accentuation on supportive equity. An assessment of these regulative changes reveals insight into the Lok Sabha's obligation to making a general set of laws that is responsive, productive, and lined up with protected standards.

1. **Modernization of Criminal Regulations:**
   The Lok Sabha's quest for modernizing criminal regulations is a vital regulative change pointed toward guaranteeing the pertinence and viability of the lawful system in tending to contemporary difficulties. This drive includes an extensive survey and change of existing rules to align them with developing cultural standards and the unique idea of crimes.
   One critical part of this administrative change is the acknowledgment that obsolete regulations may not satisfactorily address arising types of criminal

way of behaving, particularly in the computerized age. The Lok Sabha's obligation to modernization mirrors a proactive way to deal with overcome any issues between customary legitimate arrangements and the real factors of current wrongdoing.

The proposed changes incorporate refreshing and refining meanings of offenses, integrating arrangements to address cybercrimes, and dispensing with obsolete lawful ideas. The reasoning behind these progressions is established in the comprehension that a cutting edge legitimate structure should be coordinated and equipped for answering the subtleties of contemporary crimes.

Also, the modernization of criminal regulations lines up with established standards, guaranteeing that lawful arrangements are reliable with basic freedoms and global common liberties norms. This regulative change shows the Lok Sabha's obligation to maintaining law and order while cultivating a legitimate system that is simply, impartial, and receptive to the necessities of Indian culture.

2. **Public Case Strategy:**

The presentation of the Public Prosecution Strategy addresses a groundbreaking regulative change pointed toward resolving the persevering issue of case excess inside the legal framework. This strategy, formed and carried out by the Lok Sabha, connotes a guarantee to improving the productivity and viability of the law enforcement framework.

The reasoning behind this regulative change is grounded in the comprehension that defers in the goal of cases not just subvert public confidence in the overall set of laws yet in addition disregard the protected right to a fast preliminary. By focusing on the convenient goal of cases and empowering elective question goal systems, the Public Suit Strategy tries to facilitate the legal interaction and lessen the weight on conventional court procedures.

Moreover, this strategy mirrors an acknowledgment of the requirement for legal asset improvement. By smoothing out legitimate cycles and advancing elective debate goal, the Lok Sabha intends to empower the legal executive to zero in on additional mind boggling cases that require careful consultation. The regulative change encapsulated in the Public Prosecution Strategy, thusly, adds to the more extensive objectives of legal change and admittance to equity.

3. **Administrative Protections for Weak Populaces:**

The Lok Sabha's institution of regulative protections for weak populaces inside the law enforcement framework is an essential and sympathetic administrative change. This incorporates minimized networks, ladies, and kids who generally have confronted interesting difficulties inside the lawful cycle.

The reasoning behind these official changes is attached in a guarantee to correcting verifiable treacheries, tending to segregation, and giving upgraded lawful security to weak populaces. For example, regulations tending to segregation and brutality against underestimated networks are driven by the comprehension that particular lawful shields are important to safeguard these networks from fundamental predispositions and biases.

Official protections for ladies and kids mirror the Lok Sabha's obligation to tending to the one of a kind difficulties looked by these gatherings inside the law enforcement framework. Whether it is regulation pointed toward forestalling brutality against ladies or giving improved assurances to kids in struggle with the law, these administrative changes are supported by the conviction that the general set of laws should be receptive to the particular necessities and weaknesses of various sections of society.

4. **Far reaching Survey and Alteration:**

The Lok Sabha's obligation to a far reaching survey and correction of criminal regulations means a proactive regulative change pointed toward guaranteeing the proceeded with importance and viability of the lawful structure. This drive includes an intensive assessment of existing regulations, ID of holes, and tending to ambiguities that might block the effective organization of equity.

The reasoning behind this regulative change is to make a legitimate system that is clear, rational, and fit for answering the different requirements of society. By embraced a complete survey, the Lok Sabha plans to dispense with obsolete arrangements, correct irregularities, and guarantee that the overall set of laws stays a powerful device for tending to the intricacies of current wrongdoing.

This regulative change is likewise directed by a pledge to adjust the legitimate system to sacred standards and worldwide common liberties guidelines. A far reaching survey considers the ID and correction of arrangements that might be conflicting with central privileges or neglect to satisfy contemporary guidelines of equity.

5. **Authoritative Protections for Casualties:**

The Lok Sabha's accentuation on presenting regulative protections for casualties inside the law enforcement framework is a crucial change pointed toward tending to the power irregularity that frequently exists among casualties and blamed people.

These official changes, going from witness security to remuneration for casualties, mirror a promise to making a more adjusted and compassionate legitimate structure.

The reasoning behind these official protections is to give a more casualty driven approach inside the lawful structure. By instituting regulations that focus on the privileges and prosperity of casualties, the Lok Sabha expects to address the difficulties looked by casualties during legal actions, including issues connected with insurance, backing, and remuneration.

Regulative changes in such manner perceive that casualties frequently assume a vital part in the law enforcement process and ought to be treated with pride and regard. By integrating these shields into the lawful structure, the Lok Sabha looks to establish a more sympathetic and strong climate for casualties inside the law enforcement framework.

6. **Accentuation on Supportive Equity:**

The Lok Sabha's regulative accentuation on supportive equity standards addresses a change in perspective in the way to deal with law enforcement. This regulative change implies a takeoff from customary reformatory measures toward a more rehabilitative and local area situated model.

The reasoning behind this authoritative change is grounded in the conviction that tending to the underlying drivers of criminal way of behaving and elevating restoration can add to long haul cultural prosperity. Helpful equity centers around fixing the mischief brought about by criminal way of behaving and includes dynamic interest by all partners, including wrongdoers, casualties, and the local area.

Administrative changes in this space incorporate the advancement of elective question goal systems, casualty wrongdoer intervention, and local area based mediations. The Lok Sabha's obligation to integrating helpful equity standards into the legitimate system is driven by the conviction that this approach can prompt improved results regarding restoration, diminished recidivism, and local area recuperating.

This official change mirrors a guarantee to cultivating a more all encompassing and comprehensive law enforcement framework. By investigating approaches that address the hidden reasons for criminal way of behaving while at the same time including the impacted gatherings in the goal cycle, the Lok Sabha looks to make a legitimate structure that goes past corrective measures.

3.2 Analysis of the impact of these reforms on criminal laws, procedures, and penalties

The regulative changes started by the Lok Sabha to modernize the law enforcement framework in India significantly affect different angles, including criminal regulations, techniques, and punishments. This exhaustive examination digs into the repercussions of these changes, featuring the groundbreaking changes and the ramifications for the legitimate scene.

1. **Modernization of Criminal Regulations:**

   The modernization of criminal regulations, a focal point of the Lok Sabha's change plan, has fundamentally affected the legitimate system overseeing offenses in India. The changes pointed toward refreshing and adjusting existing resolutions to contemporary difficulties and cultural assumptions have brought about a more responsive and important legitimate construction.

Influence on Definitions and Offenses:

One remarkable effect is the refinement of definitions and the acquaintance of new offenses with address arising types of criminal way of behaving. The modernization endeavors have carried clearness to legitimate arrangements, guaranteeing that they precisely catch the subtleties of contemporary wrong-doing. This has, thus, improved the general set of laws' capacity to battle developing difficulties, including cybercrimes and offenses connected with innovative headways.

Arrangement with Established Standards:

The changes have additionally added to adjusting criminal regulations to sacred standards and global common freedoms principles. By killing obsolete and biased arrangements, the Lok Sabha has encouraged a legitimate structure that maintains principal freedoms, advances correspondence, and mirrors a pledge to law and order. This arrangement fortifies the established under-pinning of the law enforcement framework.

Improved Flexibility:

The modernization endeavors have blessed the legitimate structure with more prominent flexibility to changing cultural standards. The changes recognize the unique idea of society and the requirement for regulations that can successfully address new difficulties. This versatility guarantees that the overall set of laws stays an important and hearty device for keeping social control and administering equity.

2. **Public Suit Strategy:**

The presentation of the Public Suit Strategy has achieved a change in perspective in the procedural parts of the law enforcement framework. This strategy, driven by the Lok Sabha's obligation to speeding up case goal, has suggestions for the systems overseeing suit and elective debate goal.

Sped up Case Goal:

The principal effect of the Public Suit Strategy is the accentuation on sped up case goal. By focusing on the convenient removal of cases, the approach resolves the longstanding issue of build-up inside the legal framework. This affects the effectiveness of the law enforcement process, guaranteeing that a fair outcome is given on time.

Advancement of Elective Debate Goal (ADR):

The strategy's advancement of elective debate goal systems, like intercession and mediation, addresses a huge takeoff from customary case. This can possibly decongest formal court procedures, giving gatherings quicker and more savvy roads for settling debates. The effect isn't just on procedural proficiency yet in addition on cultivating a culture of consensual goal.

Asset Enhancement:

The strategy's attention on elective question goal adds to the improvement of legal assets. By redirecting specific cases from formal court procedures, the legal executive can allot its assets all the more successfully, tending to complex cases that require careful assessment. This improvement upgrades the general productivity of the law enforcement framework.

3. **Administrative Protections for Weak Populaces:**

The sanctioning of regulative shields for weak populaces inside the law enforcement framework denotes a huge step towards a more comprehensive and fair legitimate climate. These changes influence different features, including the treatment of underestimated networks, ladies, and youngsters.

Security Against Separation and Savagery:

Regulative changes tending to separation and savagery against underestimated networks act as a critical defend against verifiable treacheries. The effect is two-crease: it gives legitimate solutions for survivors of separation and savagery, and it sends serious areas of strength for an about the obligation to fairness and equity. This administrative intercession adds to the more extensive cultural objective of annihilating fundamental inclinations.

Improved Assurances for Ladies and Kids:

The changes pointed toward improving assurances for ladies and kids inside the law enforcement framework unmistakably affect legitimate strategies. The lawful scene is presently more receptive to the interesting weaknesses of these gatherings, giving instruments to their security, recovery, and redressal. This effects methods connected with the examination, preliminary, and recovery of casualties.

Inclusivity in Lawful Cycles:

The regulative protections add to making a more comprehensive lawful cycle. By perceiving and tending to the particular difficulties looked by weak populaces, the changes cultivate a climate where all people, paying little mind to foundation, can access and profit from the law enforcement framework. This inclusivity lines up with protected standards and worldwide common freedoms guidelines.

4. **Extensive Audit and Correction:**

The extensive audit and correction of criminal regulations attempted by the Lok Sabha have expansive ramifications for the lawful system's intelligence, clearness, and versatility. This change influences the actual underpinnings of the overall set of laws, impacting the procedural parts of legitimate cycles.

Clearness and Rationality:

One of the prompt effects of the far reaching survey is the improved clearness and cognizance of legitimate arrangements. Ambiguities and irregularities inside the legitimate structure are distinguished and redressed, guaranteeing that regulations are applied consistently and deciphered reliably. This adds to a lawful climate where people can all the more likely figure out their freedoms as well as certain limitations.

Flexibility to Cultural Changes:

The change's attention on versatility guarantees that the lawful system stays significant notwithstanding cultural changes. Lawful arrangements are explored to survey their appropriateness in contemporary settings, considering important changes. This flexibility is fundamental for keeping up with the viability of the general set of laws in tending to advancing difficulties.

Smoothing out Legitimate Cycles:

The exhaustive survey influences lawful methodology, smoothing out processes for more noteworthy effectiveness. Superfluous administrative obstacles and intricacies are tended to, working with smoother procedures. This smoothing out straightforwardly affects the simplicity with which people can get to the general set of laws and look for redressal for complaints.

5. **Regulative Protections for Casualties:**

The Lok Sabha's accentuation on presenting regulative shields for casualties achieves a change yet to be determined of force inside the law enforcement framework. This regulative change influences lawful methodology and punishments by putting a more noteworthy spotlight on the freedoms and prosperity of casualties.

Witness Security:

The presentation of witness security measures is a huge procedural change. By guaranteeing the wellbeing and security of witnesses, the general set of laws is better prepared to evoke honest declaration. This effects the adequacy of legal procedures by relieving the anxiety toward retaliations that witnesses might confront.

Remuneration for Casualties:

Regulative changes accommodating remuneration to casualties straightforwardly affect punishments. The general set of laws currently perceives the right of casualties to look for redressal through the indictment of guilty parties as well as through monetary pay. This comprehensive way to deal with equity thinks about the more extensive effect of wrongdoings on casualties' lives.

Casualty Driven Legitimate Cycles:

The official shields add to making lawful cycles more casualty driven. The effect is clear in lawful strategies that focus on the privileges and needs of casualties, establishing a more strong and compassionate climate inside the law enforcement framework.

6. **Accentuation on Supportive Equity:**

The Lok Sabha's official accentuation on supportive equity standards addresses a groundbreaking change in the way of thinking supporting legitimate methods and punishments. This shift influences the actual idea of discipline and the objectives of the law enforcement framework.

Elective Question Goal Instruments:

Regulative changes advancing elective question goal instruments, a vital part of supportive equity, influence lawful methods essentially. The accentuation on intercession and local area based mediations acquaints a more cooperative methodology with compromise. This effects official actions by giving roads to goal that focus on restoration over correctional measures.

Center around Restoration:

The regulative changes highlight a change in center from reformatory measures to restoration. This effects punishments by perceiving the significance of tending to the main drivers of criminal way of behaving. Lawful methodology are impacted by an expanded accentuation on renewal, decreasing recidivism, and encouraging local area recuperating.

Local area Contribution:

Supportive equity standards present the idea of local area contribution in legitimate methods. This effect is clear in the dynamic support of networks in compromise, underscoring aggregate liability and responsibility. The overall set of laws, supported by helpful equity, tries to fix the mischief brought about by criminal conduct through local area commitment.

3.3 Illustrating successful legislative changes

The Lok Sabha, India's lower place of Parliament, has led a few fruitful regulative changes pointed toward modernizing the law enforcement framework. These progressions address a critical step towards making a lawful system that is responsive, proficient, and lined up with established standards. This complete investigation digs into the fruitful regulative changes started by the Lok Sabha, representing their effect on criminal regulations, methodology, and punishments.

1. **Modernization of Criminal Regulations:**

   The Lok Sabha's obligation to modernizing criminal regulations remains as a demonstration of its ground breaking way to deal with address contemporary difficulties. Perhaps of the best authoritative change in such manner has been the complete audit and alteration of existing resolutions. This drive has modernized definitions, disposed of obsolete arrangements, and acquainted new offenses with adjust the lawful structure to the advancing idea of wrongdoing.

   Influence on Cybercrimes:

   One outstanding achievement is the joining of arrangements to address cybercrimes. The Lok Sabha perceived the rising pervasiveness of computerized offenses and answered by changing criminal regulations to incorporate an extensive variety of digital exercises. This has outfitted policing with the fundamental instruments to battle offenses, for example, hacking, online extortion, and cyberbullying, mirroring the Lok Sabha's obligation to remaining in front of mechanical progressions.

End of Prejudicial Arrangements:

The outcome of regulative changes is clear in the end of unfair arrangements inside the criminal regulations. The Lok Sabha embraced a basic assessment of existing resolutions to recognize and correct arrangements that were conflicting with sacred standards and global common freedoms guidelines. This advances correspondence under the watchful eye of the law as well as mirrors a promise to making a legitimate system that is simply, fair, and unprejudiced.

Improved Securities for Minimized People group:

Fruitful regulative changes have likewise brought about upgraded insurances for minimized networks. By tending to oppressive regulations and consolidating shields, the Lok Sabha has added to a lawful climate where people from minimized networks are better safeguarded against inclination and foul play. This achievement isn't just a legitimate achievement yet additionally a urgent step towards cultural inclusivity and value.

2. **Public Case Strategy:**

   The presentation and execution of the Public Prosecution Strategy by the Lok Sabha have achieved groundbreaking changes in legitimate methods, affecting the quick goal of cases and asset advancement inside the law enforcement framework.

   Opportune Goal of Cases:

   One of the eminent achievements of the Public Prosecution Strategy is its effect on the convenient goal of cases. By focusing on the quick removal of cases, the strategy has essentially diminished the accumulation in the legal framework. This achievement is estimated as far as mathematical decreases as well as in the substantial improvement in admittance to equity for people anticipating goal of their cases.

   Advancement of Elective Question Goal (ADR):

   The strategy's accentuation on advancing elective question goal systems has been fruitful in changing the scene of legitimate methods. The expanded utilization of intervention, discretion, and other ADR strategies has facilitated question goal as well as added to a more consensual and cooperative way to deal with compromise. This achievement means a shift towards a general set of laws that focuses on proficiency and the fulfillment of gatherings included.

   Advancement of Legal Assets:

   The Public Suit Strategy has effectively added to the improvement of legal assets. By redirecting specific cases towards elective debate goal instruments, the proper court processes are opened up to zero in on complex matters that request careful assessment. This streamlining guarantees that the legal executive works all the more effectively, tending to the main drivers of defers in legitimate methodology.

3. **Administrative Protections for Weak Populaces:**

The Lok Sabha's fruitful order of regulative protections for weak populaces inside the law enforcement framework mirrors a promise to redressing verifiable treacheries and cultivating a more fair legitimate climate.

Security Against Segregation and Savagery:

The progress of authoritative changes is obvious in the improved security against segregation and viciousness for minimized networks. The Lok Sabha's obligation to killing unfair arrangements inside the lawful structure has established a legitimate climate where people from underestimated networks can look for equity unafraid of inclination or bias. This achievement is essential for lawful value as well as for cultural inclusivity and variety.

Enabling Ladies:

Regulative shields for ladies have been especially fruitful in enabling and safeguarding them inside the law enforcement framework.

The Lok Sabha's drives, including stricter regulations against sexual offenses and improved securities for casualties, have added to a legitimate scene where ladies have a solid sense of safety and upheld. The achievement isn't just estimated in legitimate terms yet in addition in the more extensive cultural effect of advancing orientation equity.

Youngsters' Privileges and Insurances:

Effective regulative changes have likewise brought about upgraded privileges and assurances for youngsters inside the law enforcement framework. The Lok Sabha perceived the one of a kind weaknesses of kids and answered with regulations that focus on their prosperity. This achievement is obvious in lawful techniques that guarantee a youngster accommodating methodology, perceiving the significance of restoration and reintegration into society.

4. **Thorough Audit and Correction:**

The Lok Sabha's progress in endeavor an exhaustive survey and correction of criminal regulations affects legitimate systems, improving lucidity, cognizance, and versatility.

Disposal of Ambiguities:

One of the remarkable triumphs is the disposal of ambiguities inside the lawful system. The extensive audit recognized and redressed arrangements that prompted legitimate ambiguities, guaranteeing that regulations are applied consistently and deciphered reliably. This achievement adds to a general set of laws where people can explore legitimate cycles with more noteworthy lucidity and certainty.

Improved Flexibility:

The progress of the complete audit is apparent in the upgraded flexibility of the lawful structure. By intermittently surveying and revising regulations, the Lok Sabha has made a general set of laws that can really answer cultural changes and arising difficulties. This achievement guarantees that the legitimate structure stays applicable and fit for tending to the unique idea of wrongdoing and equity.

Smoothed out Legitimate Cycles:

The exhaustive audit has effectively smoothed out lawful cycles, adding to more noteworthy proficiency inside the law enforcement framework. Pointless regulatory obstacles and intricacies have been tended to, working with smoother procedures. This achievement guarantees that people can get to legitimate cycles no sweat, elevating more extensive admittance to equity.

5. **Regulative Protections for Casualties:**

   The Lok Sabha's accentuation on presenting regulative protections for casualties has been effective in rebalancing power elements inside the law enforcement framework and advancing a casualty driven approach.

Witness Assurance Measures:

One of the critical triumphs is the presentation of witness assurance measures. This regulative change guarantees the wellbeing and security of witnesses, tending to a basic hole in lawful systems. The achievement is estimated in the expanded readiness of observers to approach and affirm unafraid of retaliations, adding to additional hearty legal procedures.

Pay for Casualties:

The outcome of regulative changes accommodating remuneration to casualties is obvious in the acknowledgment of casualties' privileges to look for redressal past the arraignment of guilty parties. This comprehensive way to deal with equity thinks about the more extensive effect of wrongdoings on casualties' lives and gives an unmistakable method for help. The achievement isn't just legitimate yet in addition philanthropic, recognizing the significance of casualty compensation.

Casualty Driven Legitimate Cycles:

Authoritative shields have effectively added to making legitimate cycles more casualty driven. The effect is clear in lawful methodology that focus on the freedoms and necessities of casualties, establishing a more compassionate and strong climate inside the law enforcement framework. This achievement implies a more extensive shift towards perceiving casualties as dynamic members in the lawful cycle, as opposed to simple observers.

6. **Accentuation on Supportive Equity:**

The Lok Sabha's regulative accentuation on helpful equity standards addresses a change in perspective in the objectives of discipline and the general way of thinking of the law enforcement framework.

Elective Debate Goal Components:

One of the outstanding victories is the advancement of elective debate goal components established in supportive equity standards. The accentuation on intercession, casualty wrongdoer compromise, and local area based mediations connotes a takeoff from conventional reformatory measures. This achievement is obvious in lawful techniques that focus on restoration and local area recuperating over correctional approvals.

Center around Recovery:

The official changes highlight an effective change in center from correctional measures to recovery. By perceiving the significance of tending to the main drivers of criminal way of behaving, the Lok Sabha has added to a legitimate climate that focuses on reconstruction over simple discipline. This achievement lines up with contemporary understandings of law enforcement that underscore the potential for recovery.

Local area Association:

Supportive equity standards have effectively presented the idea of local area contribution in legitimate strategies. This effect is obvious in the dynamic support of networks in compromise, underscoring aggregate liability and responsibility. The achievement lies in encouraging a feeling of local area responsibility for processes, adding to the more extensive objective of cultural concordance.

Chapter 4

Technological Advancements

Innovative progressions have changed each part of human culture, and the law enforcement framework is no special case. In the contemporary period, the reconciliation of state of the art advancements has turned into a foundation in modernizing law enforcement works on, improving productivity, straightforwardness, and in general viability. This exhaustive examination dives into the diverse effect of innovative headways on the law enforcement framework, investigating their impact on examination methods, proof assortment, court procedures, and jail the executives.

1. **Insightful Strategies:**

   Innovative progressions have re-imagined analytical procedures, giving policing useful assets to tackle violations, distinguish culprits, and forestall crimes. One of the vital developments in this space is the utilization of criminological advances, including DNA examination, finger impression acknowledgment, and high level observation frameworks.

   Measurable Advancements:

   DNA examination, specifically, has reformed criminal examinations by giving an unrivaled degree of precision in distinguishing people.

   Progresses in DNA profiling methods have settled cold cases as well as excused wrongly charged people, highlighting the extraordinary effect of innovation on the quest for equity. Also, unique mark acknowledgment advances have become more complex, empowering policing coordinate and examine prints with more noteworthy accuracy.

   Observation Frameworks:

   The approach of cutting edge observation frameworks, like shut circuit TV (CCTV) cameras, robots, and facial acknowledgment innovation, has fundamentally expanded the abilities of policing. These advances help in checking public spaces, recognizing suspects, and forestalling crimes. Be that as it may, the utilization of facial acknowledgment innovation has raised moral worries connected with protection and likely abuse, inciting a sensitive harmony between security requirements and individual privileges.

Information Investigation and Prescient Policing:

Innovative progressions have additionally worked with the examination of tremendous measures of information to recognize examples and patterns. Prescient policing calculations use authentic wrongdoing information to anticipate expected areas of interest and distribute assets all the more proficiently. While these apparatuses hold guarantee in wrongdoing avoidance, they likewise raise worries about one-sided calculations and the potential for unfair results, stressing the requirement for moral contemplations in the sending of innovation.

2. **Proof Assortment and The executives:**

The assortment and the executives of proof are significant components of the law enforcement process, and mechanical progressions have smoothed out these cycles, offering more proficient, precise, and secure techniques.

Advanced Proof:

The multiplication of computerized advancements has prompted a remarkable expansion in computerized proof, including messages, web-based entertainment posts, and electronic correspondences. The appearance of advanced legal sciences permits specialists to extricate and dissect computerized proof, revealing urgent data in cybercrime examinations. Notwithstanding, the fast advancement of innovation likewise presents difficulties, for example, the requirement for steady updates to measurable devices and conventions to stay up with arising computerized dangers.

Body-worn Cameras:

The reception of body-worn cameras by cops addresses a huge mechanical headway in proof assortment. These gadgets record communications between policing the general population, giving a goal record of occasions. Body-worn cameras advance straightforwardness, responsibility, and can act as significant proof in criminal procedures. Be that as it may, their execution raises worries about protection, assent, and the potential for specific recording.

Blockchain Innovation:

Blockchain innovation has arisen as a solid and straightforward strategy for overseeing and safeguarding proof. Its decentralized and alter safe nature guarantees the trustworthiness of computerized proof, making it less defenseless to control or altering. This advancement tends to longstanding difficulties in proof administration and can possibly improve the unwavering quality of the law enforcement framework.

3. **Court Procedures:**

The combination of innovation in court procedures has introduced another time of effectiveness, availability, and straightforwardness. From case the board frameworks to virtual courts, these headways mean to smooth out legitimate cycles and work on the general organization of equity.

Case The executives Frameworks:

Mechanical headways on the off chance that administration frameworks have changed the manner in which courts handle regulatory assignments, case following, and archive the executives. Electronic documenting frameworks and computerized case the board stages lessen administrative work, upgrade association, and work with more proficient correspondence between court authorities, lawful experts, and different partners. This speeds up court procedures as well as decreases the gamble of mistakes related with manual record-keeping.

Virtual Courts and Distant Procedures:

The worldwide shift towards virtual correspondence advancements, advanced rapidly by the Coronavirus pandemic, has provoked the reception of virtual courts and far off procedures. Video conferencing stages take into consideration virtual hearings, witness declarations, and legitimate meetings, offering more prominent adaptability and openness. While these headways have demonstrated fundamental during seasons of emergency, they likewise present difficulties connected with innovative framework, network safety, and guaranteeing equivalent admittance to equity for all.

Electronic Court Detailing:

Electronic court detailing frameworks have supplanted conventional stenographic techniques in certain purviews. Advanced recording gadgets catch court procedures, making precise and accessible records. This improves the veracity of lawful records as well as gives an important asset to legitimate examination and case investigation.

4. **Jail The executives:**

In the domain of jail the executives, mechanical progressions have acquainted creative arrangements with address difficulties connected with security, detainee recovery, and generally speaking functional productivity.

Biometric Security Frameworks:

Biometric security frameworks, including finger impression and iris acknowledgment innovations, have become essential parts of jail the executives. These frameworks improve detainee ID, access control, and generally speaking security inside remedial offices. The execution of biometric measures adds to a safer climate while limiting the gamble of unapproved access.

Prisoner Observing and Following:

Innovative headways empower the observing and following of detainees through electronic reconnaissance frameworks. GPS-empowered lower leg screens, for instance, permit specialists to screen the developments of people released early probation, giving a more savvy and less prohibitive option in contrast to imprisonment. Notwithstanding, the utilization of such innovation raises worries about security and the potential for observation exceed.

Instructive and Recovery Projects:

Prisoner recovery programs have additionally profited from mechanical developments. Instructive stages, professional preparation programming, and e-learning drives give detained people admittance to ability building valuable open doors. These projects add to diminishing recidivism by upgrading detainees' possibilities of fruitful reintegration into society upon discharge.

5. **Moral Contemplations and Difficulties:**

While mechanical progressions offer various advantages to the law enforcement framework, they additionally raise moral contemplations and difficulties that require cautious route.

Security Concerns:

The far and wide utilization of reconnaissance advances, information investigation, and biometric frameworks raises critical security concerns. Finding some kind of harmony between open security and individual protection freedoms becomes basic, requiring hearty legitimate systems, oversight components, and straightforwardness in the sending of innovation.

Algorithmic Inclination and Decency:

The utilization of prescient policing calculations and robotized dynamic cycles presents the gamble of algorithmic inclination. Predispositions in information data sources might bring about oppressive results, excessively influencing specific networks. Guaranteeing decency and straightforwardness in algorithmic frameworks is pivotal to forestalling treacherous practices inside the law enforcement framework.

Network protection Dangers:

As innovation turns out to be more coordinated into law enforcement processes, the gamble of network safety dangers poses a potential threat. Cyberattacks on basic framework, electronic proof altering, and information breaks present critical difficulties. Fortifying network safety gauges and executing vigorous shields are fundamental to safeguard the respectability and security of the law enforcement framework.

Computerized Separation and Admittance to Equity:

The computerized partition, portrayed by differences in admittance to innovation, presents difficulties to guaranteeing equivalent admittance to equity. Remote court procedures, electronic filings, and advanced proof administration frameworks may accidentally avoid people who need admittance to the vital innovative foundation. Addressing this advanced gap is fundamental to maintain the guideline of equivalent equity under the law.

6. **Future Possibilities and Proposals:**

The direction of mechanical headways in the law enforcement framework is ready to proceed, with progressing advancements in man-made consciousness, AI, and information examination. As the scene develops, it is basic to think about future possibilities and give proposals to capable and moral joining of innovation.

Interest in Preparing and Schooling:

To bridle the maximum capacity of innovative progressions, policing, lawful experts, and legal work force should get satisfactory preparation. Preparing projects ought to zero in on the moral utilization of innovation, network protection best practices, and the capable organization of arising advancements to stay away from potentially negative results.

Foundation of Moral Rules:

The detailing and adherence to moral rules are urgent in exploring the moral contemplations related with mechanical progressions. Laying out clear moral principles for the utilization of observation advancements, prescient calculations, and computerized proof administration frameworks can assist with moderating possible maltreatments and shield individual freedoms.

Oversight and Responsibility Systems:

Vigorous oversight and responsibility components are fundamental to guarantee the mindful sending of innovation inside the law enforcement framework. Free survey sheets, standard reviews, and public straightforwardness reports can assist with considering organizations responsible for the moral utilization of innovation, consequently cultivating public trust.

Joint effort with Innovation Specialists:

Joint effort between law enforcement experts and innovation specialists is fundamental for informed navigation. Drawing in specialists in information science, network protection, and innovation regulation can assist with tending to difficulties, assess the effect of arising advancements, and guarantee that the law enforcement framework stays up with progressions while maintaining moral norms.

Local area Commitment and Inclusivity:

In the turn of events and execution of mechanical arrangements, it is basic to draw in with the networks impacted by these advancements. Guaranteeing inclusivity in the dynamic cycle can assist with recognizing possible predispositions, address concerns, and assemble trust between policing and the networks they serve.

4.1 Overview of Lok Sabha's efforts in introducing modern technology to aid law enforcement

The Lok Sabha, as the lower place of the Indian Parliament, has been instrumental in controlling the country towards modernizing its law enforcement framework by acquainting state of the art advances with help policing. The coordination of present day innovation into policing is an essential drive pointed toward improving productivity, straightforwardness, and in general viability in fighting wrongdoing. This far reaching outline digs into the Lok Sabha's endeavors in embracing and executing present day innovation, investigating the vital areas of concentration, challenges confronted, and the extraordinary effect on policing.

1. **Computerized Change in Examination Procedures:**

   The Lok Sabha's drives in utilizing present day innovation have altogether changed examination strategies utilized by policing. The reception of cutting edge measurable innovations, including DNA investigation, unique finger impression acknowledgment, and computerized criminology, has been a foundation of this change.

   DNA Examination:

   The Lok Sabha's acknowledgment of the critical job of DNA examination in criminal examinations has prompted significant interests in DNA profiling advances. High level DNA examination methods not just guide in that frame of mind with unrivaled precision yet additionally add to tackling cold cases and forestalling premature deliveries of equity. The Lok Sabha's accentuation on the significance of DNA proof highlights its obligation to using logical headways to assist policing.

   Finger impression Acknowledgment:

   The Lok Sabha's drives have likewise added to the progression of unique mark acknowledgment advances. Policing now approach more refined apparatuses for catching and examining fingerprints, improving the exactness of recognizable pieces of proof. This innovative overhaul has smoothed out the method involved with matching fingerprints, decreasing the room for mistakes and working with additional exact insightful results.

   Computerized Criminology:

   Because of the developing predominance of advanced wrongdoings, the Lok Sabha has supported the joining of computerized criminology into examination strategies.

   This incorporates the investigation of electronic proof like messages, web-based entertainment correspondences, and information put away on electronic gadgets. The Lok Sabha's acknowledgment of the meaning of computerized legal sciences mirrors a ground breaking approach in tending to the difficulties presented by cybercrimes in the contemporary period.

2. **Headways in Proof Assortment and The executives:**

   The Lok Sabha's obligation to modernizing policing to progressions in proof assortment and the executives. The acquaintance of innovations with handle computerized proof, upgrade security, and smooth out proof administration processes has been a point of convergence of these endeavors.

Advanced Proof Dealing with:

The Lok Sabha has recognized the expansion of advanced proof in criminal cases and has answered by acquainting advancements with handle this new outskirts. Policing are currently outfitted with devices and conventions for the extraction, investigation, and conservation of computerized proof. This incorporates messages, web-based entertainment content, and other electronic interchanges that have become vital parts of current examinations.

Body-worn Cameras:

The Lok Sabha plays had a crucial impact in underwriting the utilization of body-worn cameras by policemen. These gadgets act as goal witnesses, recording communications among officials and general society. This mechanical mediation upgrades straightforwardness as well as gives a dependable wellspring of proof in judicial procedures. The Lok Sabha's help for body-worn cameras lines up with the worldwide pattern towards embracing advances that encourage responsibility and confidence in policing.

Blockchain Innovation in Proof Administration:

Perceiving the requirement for secure and alter safe proof administration, the Lok Sabha has investigated the coordination of blockchain innovation. Blockchain, with its decentralized and straightforward nature, guarantees the respectability of computerized proof, decreasing the gamble of altering or control. This creative methodology mirrors the Lok Sabha's obligation to utilizing arising advancements to upgrade the unwavering quality and security of proof administration frameworks.

3. **Reinforcing Reconnaissance Frameworks:**

The Lok Sabha's endeavors to modernize policing to the fortifying of observation frameworks, furnishing organizations with cutting edge instruments to screen public spaces, distinguish thinks, and forestall crimes. While these innovations improve public security, they likewise raise significant contemplations connected with protection and moral use.

Shut Circuit TV (CCTV) Cameras:

The Lok Sabha has perceived the worth of shut circuit TV (CCTV) cameras in improving reconnaissance abilities. The essential organization of CCTV cameras openly spaces fills in as an obstruction to crimes and gives significant proof to examinations. Be that as it may, the Lok Sabha recognizes the requirement for a harmony between open wellbeing and individual protection, underlining the significance of moral contemplations in the far reaching utilization of observation advances.

Facial Acknowledgment Innovation:

The Lok Sabha's drives incorporate investigating the capability of facial acknowledgment innovation to help policing. Facial acknowledgment frameworks can help with recognizing people continuously, adding to public security endeavors. Nonetheless, the Lok Sabha is perceptive of the security concerns related with facial acknowledgment and has been effectively participated in conversations to lay out vigorous guidelines and rules for its mindful use.

Drone Innovation:

The Lok Sabha has likewise thought to be the combination of robot innovation for observation purposes. Drones give policing a flexible and spry instrument for observing enormous regions, answering crises, and leading pursuit and salvage tasks. The Lok Sabha's investigation of robot innovation mirrors a familiarity with the advancing scene of observation devices and the requirement for versatile and dependable use.

4. **Advanced Change in Court Procedures:**

Notwithstanding progressions in analytical strategies and proof administration, the Lok Sabha has led computerized changes in court procedures. The presentation of current advancements in courts plans to smooth out processes, upgrade availability, and guarantee the effective organization of equity.

Electronic Case The executives Frameworks:

The Lok Sabha's obligation to digitizing court procedures is apparent in the execution of electronic case the executives frameworks. These frameworks work with the consistent following of cases, electronic documenting, and effective correspondence between partners. The change from manual record-keeping to advanced case the board has fundamentally decreased desk work, limited mistakes, and assisted regulatory assignments inside the overall set of laws.

Virtual Courts and Distant Procedures:

The Lok Sabha plays had a critical impact in advancing virtual courts and distant procedures, especially because of the difficulties presented by the Coronavirus pandemic. Video conferencing stages have been embraced to lead virtual hearings, witness declarations, and legitimate meetings.

This innovation not just guarantees coherence in that frame of mind during emergencies yet in addition improves availability for defendants, lawful experts, and different members.

Computerized Court Revealing:

Computerized court revealing frameworks have supplanted conventional stenographic techniques in certain purviews. Computerized recording gadgets catch court procedures, producing precise and accessible records. This innovative update improves the exactness of legitimate records as well as gives an important asset to lawful examination and case investigation.

5. **Mechanical Developments in Jail The executives:**

The Lok Sabha's obligation to utilizing current innovation reaches out to the domain of jail the executives, where inventive arrangements are acquainted with address security concerns, upgrade prisoner restoration, and work on by and large functional productivity.

Biometric Security Frameworks:

Biometric security frameworks, including unique mark and iris acknowledgment advances, have become indispensable parts of jail the executives. These frameworks upgrade prisoner ID, access control, and by and large security inside restorative offices. The Lok Sabha's underwriting of biometric measures mirrors a proactive way to deal with modernizing jail security and limiting the gamble of unapproved access.

Detainee Checking and Following:

Mechanical progressions empower the observing and following of detainees through electronic reconnaissance frameworks. GPS-empowered lower leg screens, for example, permit specialists to screen the developments of people released early probation. This innovation gives a more practical and less prohibitive option in contrast to imprisonment. Be that as it may, the Lok Sabha recognizes the need to address protection concerns and guarantee mindful utilization of such checking advancements.

Instructive and Recovery Projects:

The Lok Sabha perceives the job of innovation in working with instructive and recovery programs for detainees. Computerized stages, professional preparation programming, and e-learning drives offer imprisoned people potential open doors for ability improvement and schooling. These projects add to decreasing recidivism by improving prisoners' possibilities of effective reintegration into society upon discharge.

6. **Tending to Moral Contemplations and Difficulties:**

The Lok Sabha's endeavors in acquainting present day innovation with help policing joined by a guarantee to tending to moral contemplations and difficulties. As innovation turns out to be all the more profoundly coordinated into the law enforcement framework, the Lok Sabha perceives the significance of exploring expected entanglements and defending individual freedoms.

Protection Concerns:

The Lok Sabha recognizes the significance of protection and is effectively participated in conversations encompassing the moral utilization of observation advances. Finding some kind of harmony between guaranteeing public security and safeguarding individual protection privileges is vital. The Lok Sabha is focused on laying out clear guidelines and rules to administer the dependable arrangement of observation innovations.

Algorithmic Predisposition and Decency:

With regards to prescient policing calculations and mechanized direction, the Lok Sabha perceives the potential for algorithmic inclination. Guaranteeing decency and straightforwardness in algorithmic frameworks is a key thought. The Lok Sabha is effectively investigating measures to relieve predispositions and forestall unfair results, encouraging public confidence in the moral utilization of innovation.

Online protection Dangers:

The Lok Sabha is aware of the online protection dangers that go with the combination of innovation into policing. Shielding against cyberattacks, information breaks, and proof altering is really important. The Lok Sabha is effectively attempting to fortify online protection measures, guaranteeing the honesty and security of the law enforcement framework.

Advanced Gap and Admittance to Equity:

The Lok Sabha recognizes the advanced gap and the potential for inconsistent admittance to equity. Endeavors are in progress to address differences in admittance to innovation, guaranteeing that remote court procedures, electronic filings, and advanced proof administration frameworks are open to all portions of society. Connecting the computerized partition is fundamental for maintaining the rule of equivalent equity under the law.

7. **Future Possibilities and Suggestions:**

The Lok Sabha's drives in acquainting current innovation with help policing India on a direction towards a mechanically progressed and effective law enforcement framework. Looking forward, the Lok Sabha thinks about future possibilities and gives suggestions for capable and moral incorporation of innovation.

Interest in Preparing and Training:

To expand the advantages of mechanical headways, the Lok Sabha underlines the significance of interest in preparing and training. Policing, legitimate specialists, and legal staff should get thorough preparation on the moral utilization of innovation, network safety best practices, and the capable organization of arising advances.

Foundation of Moral Rules:

Perceiving the requirement for moral principles, the Lok Sabha is effectively engaged with the foundation of clear rules overseeing the utilization of innovation in policing. Moral rules will act as a structure for guaranteeing mindful and fair works on, limiting the gamble of misuses and maintaining individual freedoms.

Oversight and Responsibility Instruments:

The Lok Sabha advocates for powerful oversight and responsibility components to screen the arrangement of innovation in policing. Autonomous survey sheets, customary reviews, and public straightforwardness reports are fundamental parts of these systems. Guaranteeing responsibility encourages public confidence in the moral utilization of innovation.

Coordinated effort with Innovation Specialists:

Perceiving the powerful idea of innovation, the Lok Sabha stresses the significance of coordinated effort with innovation specialists. Connecting with specialists in information science, network protection, and innovation regulation will work with informed direction, address difficulties, and guarantee that the law enforcement framework stays versatile and moral.

Local area Commitment and Inclusivity:

In the turn of events and execution of mechanical arrangements, the Lok Sabha highlights the meaning of local area commitment and inclusivity. Drawing in with the networks impacted by these advancements distinguishes possible predispositions, address concerns, and construct trust between policing and the general population.

4.2 Discussion on the implementation of digital platforms, artificial intelligence, and data analytics

The execution of computerized stages, man-made brainpower (man-made intelligence), and information examination in the law enforcement framework addresses a change in outlook in the manner in which policing work, break down data, and simply decide. This far reaching conversation investigates the diverse effect of these advances, analyzing their expected advantages, moral contemplations, challenges, and the groundbreaking ramifications for the organization of equity.

1. **Computerized Stages in Policing:**

   Computerized stages have arisen as fundamental devices in present day policing, processes, improving correspondence, and giving a unified store to basic data. The execution of advanced stages incorporates different viewpoints, including case the executives frameworks, correspondence organizations, and data sharing stages.

   Case The board Frameworks:

   The reception of computerized case the board frameworks by policing has altered how cases are taken care of. These frameworks work with the electronic recording of case reports, track the advancement of examinations, and empower consistent joint effort among policing. The Lok Sabha's help for computerized case the executives mirrors a guarantee to proficiency and straightforwardness inside the law enforcement framework.

   Correspondence Organizations:

   Computerized stages assume a critical part in further developing correspondence networks among policing at neighborhood, local, and public levels. Secure correspondence channels, scrambled informing frameworks, and ongoing cooperation stages empower quick and effective data trade. This interconnectedness improves the capacity of policing answer immediately to arising dangers and direction endeavors across locales.

   Data Sharing Stages:

The Lok Sabha's drives incorporate the foundation of data sharing stages that empower various organizations to share pertinent information and knowledge. These stages add to a more all encompassing comprehension of crimes, work with joint examinations, and upgrade the general viability of policing. In any case, the Lok Sabha perceives the need to offset data imparting to protection contemplations and is effectively taken part in forming rules to oversee the capable utilization of these stages.

2. **Man-made reasoning in Policing:**

Computerized reasoning, with its capacity to break down huge measures of information, recognize examples, and make forecasts, has turned into a groundbreaking power in policing. The Lok Sabha's investigation of computer based intelligence applications in the law enforcement framework mirrors a ground breaking way to deal with tending to complex difficulties.

Prescient Policing:

One huge utilization of computer based intelligence is prescient policing, where calculations dissect verifiable wrongdoing information to recognize expected areas of interest and examples. The Lok Sabha's thought of prescient policing mirrors an affirmation of the expected advantages in asset enhancement and wrongdoing counteraction. Notwithstanding, the Lok Sabha is additionally mindful of worries connected with algorithmic predisposition and possible unfair results, highlighting the significance of fair and straightforward computer based intelligence frameworks.

Facial Acknowledgment Innovation:

The Lok Sabha's conversation on the execution of facial acknowledgment innovation features the capability of man-made intelligence in recognizing people progressively.

Facial acknowledgment frameworks help policing distinguishing suspects, improving public security, and forestalling crimes. In any case, the Lok Sabha is effectively participated in thoughts on moral rules and guidelines to address protection concerns and possible abuse of this innovation.

Insightful Help:

Simulated intelligence fueled apparatuses offer insightful help by investigating computerized proof, distinguishing associations among people and elements, and revealing secret examples. The Lok Sabha's acknowledgment of artificial intelligence's job in insightful cycles mirrors a comprehension of the productivity gains and upgraded capacities it brings to policing. By the by, conversations inside the Lok Sabha stress the requirement for shields to forestall misuse and guarantee the capable utilization of simulated intelligence in criminal examinations.

3. **Information Examination in Law enforcement:**

Information examination, powered by the remarkable development of computerized data, has turned into a foundation in the modernization of the law enforcement framework. The Lok Sabha's conversations on information examination highlight its capability to infer experiences, illuminate direction, and upgrade the general effectiveness of policing.

Wrongdoing Investigation and Avoidance:

Information investigation apparatuses empower policing to break down wrongdoing patterns, recognize designs, and convey assets decisively. The Lok Sabha's help for information driven wrongdoing examination mirrors a pledge to proactive measures in forestalling crimes. Notwithstanding, conversations inside the Lok Sabha likewise stress the requirement for dependable information administration to address protection concerns and guarantee consistence with legitimate principles.

Risk Appraisal and Condemning:

Information examination assumes a part in risk appraisal devices utilized in the law enforcement framework to assess factors impacting condemning and parole choices. The Lok Sabha's thought of these apparatuses mirrors a familiarity with their likely effect on reasonableness and equity. The Lok Sabha effectively takes part in conversations to guarantee that these devices are straightforward, impartial, and lined up with established standards.

Asset Allotment and Effectiveness:

The Lok Sabha recognizes the job of information examination in advancing asset allotment inside the law enforcement framework. By dissecting functional information, offices can recognize regions for development, distribute assets all the more really, and smooth out processes. The Lok Sabha's help for information driven direction mirrors a pledge to upgrading the productivity of policing.

4. **Advantages of Execution:**

The execution of computerized stages, man-made brainpower, and information examination in the law enforcement framework achieves a scope of potential advantages that add to productivity, straightforwardness, and the general viability of policing.

Effective Data The board:

Computerized stages smooth out data the board by giving an incorporated vault to case records, proof, and knowledge. This productivity diminishes desk work, limits mistakes, and upgrades the openness of basic data for policing. The Lok Sabha's help for advanced stages lines up determined to enhance data the executives inside the law enforcement framework.

Improved Insightful Capacities:

The mix of simulated intelligence in analytical cycles upgrades policing to dissect huge measures of information, recognize designs, and create noteworthy experiences. This prompts more compelling and designated examinations, adding to the opportune goal of cases. The Lok Sabha's investigation of man-made intelligence applications mirrors a comprehension of the potential for mechanical headways to reinforce insightful endeavors.

Proactive Wrongdoing Avoidance:

Prescient policing, worked with by computer based intelligence, empowers policing to adopt a proactive strategy to wrongdoing counteraction. By distinguishing possible areas of interest and examples, organizations can convey assets prudently, preventing crimes and improving public security. The Lok Sabha's thought of prescient policing mirrors a guarantee to tackling innovation for safeguard measures inside networks.

Information Driven Navigation:

The utilization of information examination in dynamic cycles enables policing to pursue informed and proof based choices. From asset assignment to vital preparation, information driven dynamic upgrades the general proficiency of policing. The Lok Sabha's help for information investigation lines up with the target of cultivating a culture of informed dynamic inside the law enforcement framework.

5. **Moral Contemplations and Difficulties:**

   While the execution of computerized stages, artificial intelligence, and information investigation offers huge advantages, it additionally raises moral contemplations and difficulties that request cautious examination and guideline. The Lok Sabha's conversations on these innovations incorporate a guarantee to tending to moral worries and moderating expected chances.

Security Contemplations:

The assortment, examination, and sharing of tremendous measures of information raise huge security concerns. The Lok Sabha perceives the need to find some kind of harmony between the advantages of innovation and defending individual protection freedoms.

Conversations inside the Lok Sabha underscore the significance of powerful guidelines and rules to guarantee dependable information rehearses and safeguard residents' protection.

Algorithmic Predisposition and Reasonableness:

The utilization of artificial intelligence calculations presents the gamble of predisposition, possibly prompting oppressive results. The Lok Sabha recognizes the significance of reasonableness in algorithmic frameworks and is effectively taken part in conversations to lay out rules that forestall predispositions and advance straightforwardness. Guaranteeing that man-made intelligence frameworks line up with sacred standards is a critical thought inside the Lok Sabha's considerations.

Security Dangers and Digital Dangers:

The dependence on computerized stages and information investigation presents security dangers and weaknesses. The Lok Sabha is mindful of the potential for digital dangers, information breaks, and unapproved access. Progressing conversations accentuate the requirement for strong network safety measures to shield the respectability of data and safeguard against noxious exercises.

Lawful and Administrative System:

The quick advancement of innovation frequently dominates the improvement of lawful and administrative systems. The Lok Sabha perceives the requirement for extensive regulation and guidelines to oversee the utilization of advanced stages, simulated intelligence, and information examination in the law enforcement framework. These conversations mean to lay out an unmistakable legitimate system that guarantees responsibility, straightforwardness, and adherence to sacred standards.

6. **Groundbreaking Ramifications for the Organization of Equity:**

The execution of advanced stages, computer based intelligence, and information examination has groundbreaking ramifications for the organization of equity, reshaping customary cycles, and acquainting imaginative methodologies with policing judicial actions.

Informed Direction:

The utilization of information examination empowers informed decision-production at different phases of the law enforcement framework. From policing to court procedures, the accessibility of information driven bits of knowledge upgrades the capacity of partners to go with choices in view of proof and patterns. This extraordinary shift adds to a more productive and responsible organization of equity.

Effectiveness Gains and Asset Streamlining:

Advanced stages and simulated intelligence add to effectiveness gains by improving asset assignment, smoothing out cycles, and diminishing manual responsibilities.

This groundbreaking effect prompts more powerful policing, more limited case handling times, and worked on generally speaking proficiency inside the law enforcement framework. The Lok Sabha's help for these innovations mirrors a promise to modernizing and improving the viability of equity organization.

Proactive Wrongdoing Counteraction and Public Wellbeing:

The extraordinary ramifications stretch out to the proactive counteraction of wrongdoings through prescient policing and improved reconnaissance abilities. By utilizing innovation to recognize expected dangers and criminal examples, policing can go to preplanned lengths, adding to public security. The Lok Sabha's investigation of these extraordinary methodologies lines up fully intent on making more secure networks.

Challenges in Transformation and Execution:

The extraordinary ramifications additionally acquire difficulties terms of transformation and execution. Policing and legitimate experts might confront obstacles in adjusting to new advances, and there might be protection from change. The Lok Sabha's conversations envelop methodologies to address these difficulties, including preparing programs, partner commitment, and staged execution draws near.

4.3 Evaluation of the benefits and challenges of technological integration

The combination of innovation into the law enforcement framework delivers a bunch of advantages and difficulties, reshaping the scene of policing, procedures, and remedies. This extensive assessment investigates the multi-layered parts of innovative combination, gauging the benefits it offers against the difficulties it presents. The Lok Sabha's commitment with this assessment mirrors a nuanced comprehension of the perplexing elements related with utilizing innovation chasing a modernized and viable law enforcement framework.

Advantages of Innovative Combination:

Upgraded Effectiveness and Efficiency:

Innovative combination smoothes out functional cycles inside the law enforcement framework, prompting upgraded effectiveness and efficiency. Computerized stages, simulated intelligence calculations, and information investigation instruments robotize routine errands, lessen administrative work, and advance asset portion. This proficiency gains convert into faster case handling, worked on insightful results, and generally efficiency gains for policing and legitimate professionals.

Further developed Data The executives:

The joining of advanced stages works with further developed data the executives across the law enforcement framework. Electronic case the executives frameworks, secure correspondence organizations, and data sharing stages make a brought together storehouse for case reports, proof, and insight. This concentrated methodology guarantees that applicable data is effectively available to approved staff, adding to more educated direction.

High level Analytical Capacities:

Innovative coordination improves insightful abilities through apparatuses, for example, artificial intelligence controlled investigation and computerized legal sciences. Prescient policing calculations assist policing distinguishing wrongdoing areas of interest, while computerized legal sciences devices help in the examination of electronic proof. These high level abilities engage agents to settle cases all the more productively, recognize examples, and remain in front of arising dangers.

Proactive Wrongdoing Anticipation:

Prescient policing, empowered by computer based intelligence, permits policing take a proactive position in forestalling violations. By dissecting verifiable information and distinguishing designs, offices can convey assets decisively to likely areas of interest, discouraging crimes before they happen. This preventive methodology adds to public wellbeing and lines up with the Lok Sabha's vision for a more secure and safer society.

Information Driven Independent direction:

The utilization of information investigation devices works with information driven decision-production at different levels of the law enforcement framework. From policing to court procedures, partners can depend on proof based experiences got from information investigation. This extraordinary shift adds to more educated and objective direction, lessening the probability of blunders and upgrading the general nature of equity organization.

Improved Public Wellbeing:

The combination of innovation adds to upgraded public wellbeing by further developing observation abilities, smoothing out crisis reaction frameworks, and working with speedy distinguishing proof of expected dangers. Shut circuit TV (CCTV) cameras, facial acknowledgment innovation, and ongoing correspondence stages all assume a part in establishing a more secure climate for residents. The Lok Sabha's underwriting of these innovations lines up with its obligation to shielding the prosperity of general society.

Difficulties of Mechanical Reconciliation:

Protection Concerns:

One of the essential difficulties related with mechanical joining in the law enforcement framework is the possible encroachment on security privileges.

The assortment, investigation, and sharing of immense measures of individual information raise worries about unjustifiable reconnaissance and the abuse of touchy data. The Lok Sabha perceives the significance of offsetting public security with individual protection privileges and is effectively participated in planning guidelines and rules to address these worries.

Algorithmic Predisposition and Decency:

The utilization of computer based intelligence calculations presents the gamble of predisposition, possibly prompting biased results. Prescient policing calculations, facial acknowledgment innovation, and other computer based intelligence controlled apparatuses may show predispositions that lopsidedly influence specific networks. The Lok Sabha recognizes the requirement for reasonableness in algorithmic frameworks and stresses the significance of rules to forestall predispositions and guarantee straightforwardness in the organization of these advances.

Network protection Dangers:

The dependence on computerized stages and interconnected frameworks uncovered the law enforcement framework to network protection dangers. Information breaks, unapproved access, and other digital dangers present dangers to the respectability of data and the general working of the framework. The Lok Sabha is effectively engaged with conversations to fortify network safety measures, guaranteeing that mechanical incorporation doesn't think twice about security of delicate information.

Lawful and Administrative System:

The quick speed of innovative progressions frequently dominates the improvement of an exhaustive legitimate and administrative system. This hole brings difficulties up in guaranteeing that the utilization of innovation lines up with lawful norms and established standards. The Lok Sabha perceives the requirement for powerful regulation and guidelines to administer mechanical incorporation, giving clear rules to capable and moral use.

Advanced Separation and Admittance to Equity:

The inconsistent admittance to innovation, known as the computerized partition, represents a test in guaranteeing that the advantages of mechanical combination are open to all sections of society. Abberations in admittance to advanced stages, online court procedures, and electronic proof administration frameworks might add to inconsistent admittance to equity. The Lok Sabha is effectively addressing these abberations to connect the computerized partition and maintain the rule of equivalent equity under the law.

Protection from Change and Preparing Needs:

The presentation of new advancements might confront obstruction from inside the law enforcement framework, including policing, legitimate experts, and court staff. Protection from change can obstruct the compelling execution of mechanical arrangements.Moreover, there is a requirement for far reaching preparing projects to outfit partners with the abilities expected to dependably explore and use these innovations. The Lok Sabha perceives the significance of addressing these difficulties to guarantee a smooth change to a mechanically progressed framework.

Adjusting Advantages and Difficulties:

The Lok Sabha's commitment with the advantages and difficulties of innovative combination mirrors a pledge to finding some kind of harmony between utilizing the benefits presented by innovation and relieving expected gambles. The extraordinary capability of innovation is clear in the proficiency gains, worked on analytical capacities, and proactive wrongdoing anticipation it brings to the law enforcement framework. In any case, the Lok Sabha is similarly mindful of the moral contemplations and difficulties that request cautious guideline and oversight.

Guaranteeing Moral Utilization of Innovation:

The Lok Sabha's conversations accentuate the significance of guaranteeing the moral utilization of innovation inside the law enforcement framework. Tending to security concerns, forestalling algorithmic predispositions, and shielding against network safety dangers are key to the Lok Sabha's obligation to maintaining individual privileges and sacred standards. The plan of clear guidelines and rules, directed by moral contemplations, is a vital focal point of the Lok Sabha's drives.

Local area Commitment and Inclusivity:

Perceiving the likely effect of mechanical combination on networks, the Lok Sabha effectively advocates for local area commitment and inclusivity in the dynamic cycle. Drawing in with networks impacted by these advancements recognizes expected predispositions, address concerns, and fabricate trust between policing and people in general. The Lok Sabha's obligation to inclusivity lines up with the standards of popularity based administration and participatory navigation.

Interest in Preparing and Schooling:

To augment the advantages of mechanical coordination, the Lok Sabha highlights the significance of interest in preparing and schooling. Policing, legitimate professionals, and legal work force should get exhaustive preparation on the moral utilization of innovation, network safety best practices, and the mindful organization of arising advances. Preparing programs add to building a talented labor force equipped for exploring the intricacies of an innovatively driven law enforcement framework.

Oversight and Responsibility Systems:

The Lok Sabha perceives the requirement for vigorous oversight and responsibility components to guarantee the capable arrangement of innovation inside the law enforcement framework. Free survey sheets, ordinary reviews, and public straightforwardness reports are fundamental parts of these instruments. Guaranteeing responsibility encourages public confidence in the moral utilization of innovation and lines up with the Lok Sabha's obligation to straightforwardness and responsibility in administration.

Chapter 5

Strengthening Law Enforcement Agencies

Reinforcing policing is a basic part of building a viable and versatile law enforcement framework. This extensive conversation investigates the multi-layered systems and drives pointed toward improving the abilities, assets, and in general adequacy of policing in India. The Lok Sabha's obligation to fortifying policing a comprehensive way to deal with address the developing difficulties and requests of keeping up with public wellbeing and maintaining law and order.

1. **Limit Building and Preparing:**

   A foundation of reinforcing policing is putting resources into limit building and preparing programs. The Lok Sabha perceives the unique idea of wrongdoing and the requirement for policing to be furnished with the most recent abilities, information, and apparatuses. Exhaustive preparation programs envelop regions, for example, insightful procedures, crime scene investigation, advanced education, local area policing, and the moral utilization of innovation. The Lok Sabha's help for consistent preparation guarantees that policing are ready to address arising difficulties and maintain the best expectations of impressive skill.

2. **Enrollment and Staff The executives:**

   Guaranteeing the enrollment of qualified and various faculty is crucial for the viability of policing. The Lok Sabha's drives center around laying out straightforward and merit-based enrollment processes that draw in people with the important abilities and respectability. Moreover, faculty the executives procedures, including fair advancements, execution assessments, and psychological well-being support, add to keeping a spurred and fit policing. The Lok Sabha's obligation to staff the executives lines up determined to encourage a positive and responsible hierarchical culture.

3. **Innovative Incorporation:**

The Lok Sabha recognizes the extraordinary job of innovation in improving policing. Drives to coordinate state of the art advances, for example, man-made consciousness, information examination, and computerized legal sciences, engage policing to adjust to the developing idea of wrongdoing. The Lok Sabha's help for mechanical reconciliation mirrors a pledge to furnishing policing the instruments important to direct productive examinations, investigate information, and forestall and answer crimes successfully.

4. **Local area Policing and Commitment:**

Local area policing is a procedure that stresses coordinated effort between policing and the networks they serve. The Lok Sabha perceives the significance of cultivating positive connections between policing general society. Local area policing drives include proactive commitment with local area individuals, tending to nearby worries, and building trust. The Lok Sabha's underwriting of local area policing lines up with the rule of comprehensive and participatory policing mirrors the requirements and upsides of different networks.

5. **Foundation and Asset Distribution:**

Guaranteeing that policing have satisfactory foundation and assets is fundamental for their functional adequacy. The Lok Sabha's drives incorporate vital asset distribution to give policing present day hardware, vehicles, and offices. This guarantees that faculty have the important apparatuses to proficiently complete their obligations. Moreover, the Lok Sabha stresses the requirement for standard appraisals to recognize holes in framework and address them to upgrade generally speaking functional limit.

6. **Key Associations and Interagency Joint effort:**

The Lok Sabha perceives the significance of encouraging key organizations and advancing joint effort among various policing. Interagency coordination upgrades the sharing of insight, assets, and aptitude. The Lok Sabha's help for cooperative endeavors guarantees a bound together and composed reaction to complex difficulties, including coordinated wrongdoing, psychological warfare, and digital dangers. By advancing collaborations among different offices, the Lok Sabha adds to a more powerful and interconnected policing.

7. **Lawful Changes and Strengthening:**

Legitimate changes assume a critical part in engaging policing to battle wrongdoing inside the limits of law and order successfully. The Lok Sabha's commitment with legitimate changes incorporates refreshing and reinforcing existing regulation, furnishing policing the important lawful devices to address arising dangers. Guaranteeing that regulations are clear, forward-thinking, and lined up with protected standards engages policing to complete their obligations with certainty and authenticity.

8. **Wrongdoing Anticipation and Public Mindfulness:**

   The Lok Sabha perceives the significance of proactive wrongdoing anticipation procedures. Drives to raise public mindfulness about wrongdoing counteraction and security add to making a careful and informed populace. The Lok Sabha's accentuation on local area schooling programs, public mindfulness missions, and organizations with non-legislative associations mirrors a guarantee to including people in general as dynamic accomplices in the general wellbeing and security of society.

9. **Responsibility and Oversight Instruments:**

   Guaranteeing responsibility and straightforwardness inside policing is principal to keeping up with public trust. The Lok Sabha upholds the foundation of hearty oversight systems, including autonomous survey sheets, inward issues units, and outer reviews. These systems consider policing responsible for their activities, forestall maltreatment of force, and add to a culture of impressive skill and honesty inside the organizations.

10. **Tending to Emotional wellness and Prosperity:**

    Perceiving the difficult idea of policing, the Lok Sabha focuses on drives that address the emotional well-being and prosperity of policing. Emotional well-being support programs, advising administrations, and stress the board assets add to keeping up with the mental versatility of cops. The Lok Sabha's obligation to the psychological well-being of work force mirrors an all encompassing way to deal with reinforcing the general prosperity of those entrusted with guaranteeing public security.

11. **Worldwide Joint effort:**

    In an undeniably interconnected world, the Lok Sabha recognizes the significance of worldwide joint effort in tending to transnational wrongdoings and worldwide security challenges. Participating in cooperative endeavors with worldwide policing, taking part in joint activities, and sharing prescribed procedures add to India's capacity to answer really to cross-line dangers. The Lok Sabha's help for worldwide cooperation highlights its obligation to an aggregate and worldwide way to deal with policing.

12. **Legitimate Guide and Admittance to Equity:**

    Guaranteeing admittance to equity for all residents is a major rule of the law enforcement framework.

    The Lok Sabha's drives incorporate measures to improve lawful guide administrations, especially for helpless and underestimated populaces. Offering legitimate help guarantees that people, no matter what their financial status, possess the ability to protect their freedoms and get a fair preliminary. The Lok Sabha's obligation to admittance to equity lines up with the standards of uniformity and decency.

13. **Reaction to Arising Dangers:**

The Lok Sabha perceives the powerful idea of arising dangers, including cyber-crime, illegal intimidation, and capricious types of crime. Drives to upgrade policing to answer these dangers imply specific preparation, mechanical progressions, and key associations with online protection specialists and worldwide offices. The Lok Sabha's proactive way to deal with addressing arising dangers mirrors its obligation to remaining in front of developing difficulties.

5.1 Initiatives aimed at enhancing the capabilities of police forces

Improving the capacities of police powers is a basic part of guaranteeing public wellbeing, keeping up with peace and lawfulness, and maintaining law and order. The Lok Sabha's obligation to these objectives is reflected in a progression of drives pointed toward outfitting police powers with the fundamental devices, abilities, and assets to successfully address the developing difficulties in the public eye. This thorough conversation investigates the key drives attempted by the Lok Sabha to upgrade the capacities of police powers in India.

1. **Preparing and Ability Advancement:**

   A fundamental drive in improving police capacities is the accentuation on complete preparation and expertise improvement programs. Perceiving that compelling policing requires a different arrangement of abilities, the Lok Sabha advocates for continuous preparation in regions, for example, swarm the board, emergency reaction, de-heightening methods, local area policing, and the moral utilization of power. By putting resources into the persistent improvement of police faculty, the Lok Sabha guarantees that officials are good to go to deal with a scope of circumstances with impressive skill and capability.

2. **Modernizing Hardware and Innovation:**

   The Lok Sabha recognizes the groundbreaking effect of current innovation on policing. Drives to modernize police gear and innovation incorporate the arrangement of cutting edge correspondence frameworks, reconnaissance devices, scientific innovation, and computerized proof administration frameworks. The joining of innovation not just upgrades the analytical capacities of police powers yet in addition works on their generally functional proficiency. The Lok Sabha's help for mechanical progression lines up with the vision of making innovatively proficient and responsive police powers.

3. **Local area Policing Drives:**

   Perceiving the significance of building trust and coordinated effort between police powers and the networks they serve, the Lok Sabha advances local area policing drives. Local area policing includes proactive commitment with neighborhood networks, grasping their requirements, and including residents in the plan and execution of policing methodologies. This approach encourages a feeling of shared liability regarding public security and adds to a good connection between the police and the general population.

4. **Particular Units and Teams:**

   To address explicit difficulties and arising dangers, the Lok Sabha upholds the foundation of specific units and teams inside police powers. These units might zero in on regions like cybercrime, counter-psychological oppression, coordinated wrongdoing, and opiates. By making specific units, police powers can foster mastery specifically spaces, guaranteeing a more designated and successful reaction to complex and developing crimes.

5. **Interest in Scientific Capacities:**

   Compelling criminal examinations require powerful measurable capacities. The Lok Sabha perceives the significance of putting resources into scientific innovation and foundation to upgrade the capacity of police powers to gather, examine, and present proof. This incorporates the foundation of criminolog-ical research facilities outfitted with cutting edge instruments for DNA in-vestigation, fingerprinting, ballistics, and other measurable assessments. The Lok Sabha's drives in such manner add to the logical and proof based way to deal with criminal examinations.

6. **Further developing Knowledge Assembling and Sharing:**

   Even with different and refined crimes, knowledge assembling and sharing assume a vital part in policing. The Lok Sabha accentuates drives to upgrade knowledge abilities, including the utilization of cutting edge information examination, data sharing stages, and joint effort with insight organizations. By working on the progression of noteworthy knowledge, police powers can expect and answer dangers all the more really.

7. **Advancing Orientation Awareness and Variety:**

   Perceiving the significance of a different and orientation touchy police force, the Lok Sabha advocates for drives pointed toward advancing inclusivity in-side policing. This incorporates endeavors to enroll more ladies into the police force, give orientation delicate preparation, and address issues connected with the portrayal of minimized gatherings. A different and orientation delicate police force is better prepared to comprehend and address the requirements of all fragments of society.

8. **Reinforcing Cybercrime Units:**

   The Lok Sabha recognizes the developing danger of cybercrime and the re-quirement for specific abilities to battle it. Drives incorporate the foundation and reinforcing of devoted cybercrime units inside police powers. These units are prepared to explore wrongdoings like internet based misrepresentation, hacking, and advanced dangers. The Lok Sabha's help for cybercrime units mirrors a ground breaking way to deal with tending to the difficulties pre-sented by the computerized scene.

9. **Upgrading Police Government assistance and Prosperity:**

The prosperity of police faculty is essential to their adequacy and flexibility. The Lok Sabha perceives this and supports drives pointed toward upgrading police government assistance, including further developed lodging offices, admittance to medical services, emotional well-being support projects, and measures to address word related pressure. By focusing on the prosperity of police faculty, the Lok Sabha guarantees a more persuaded and competent labor force.

10. **Guaranteeing Responsibility and Incredible skill:**

The Lok Sabha puts serious areas of strength for an on responsibility and incredible skill inside police powers. Drives incorporate the foundation of inward undertakings units, ordinary execution assessments, and systems for tending to wrongdoing and debasement. By encouraging a culture of responsibility and incredible skill, the Lok Sabha guarantees that police powers work with honesty and maintain the best expectations of moral lead.

11. **Advancing People group Effort and Commitment:**

Viable policing includes dynamic commitment with the networks being served. The Lok Sabha upholds drives that advance local area outreach, including public mindfulness crusades, intuitive projects, and associations with neighborhood associations. Drawing in with networks constructs trust, works with correspondence, and urges residents to effectively take part in guaranteeing their own security.

12. **Tending to Dealing and Kid Security:**

Perceiving the weaknesses of ladies and kids to different types of double-dealing, the Lok Sabha upholds drives pointed toward tending to illegal exploitation and guaranteeing youngster security. Particular units inside police powers center around forestalling and examining instances of dealing, while endeavors are made to reinforce youngster insurance units. These drives line up with the Lok Sabha's obligation to protecting the most weak citizenry.

13. **Ordinary Survey and Appraisal:**

Ceaseless improvement is a vital part of upgrading police capacities. The Lok Sabha upholds customary audits and evaluations of police execution, functional procedures, and the adequacy of carried out drives. These assessments assist with recognizing regions for development, survey the effect of new approaches, and guarantee that police powers stay versatile and receptive to advancing difficulties.

14. **Legitimate Changes and Strengthening:**

Enabling police powers includes furnishing them with the legitimate devices important to really complete their obligations while maintaining protected standards. The Lok Sabha's commitment with lawful changes incorporates refreshing and reinforcing existing regulation to line up with contemporary difficulties. This incorporates resolving issues like custodial freedoms, procedural decency, and the insurance of basic liberties. Enabling police powers inside an unmistakable lawful system guarantees that they can complete their obligations with certainty and authenticity.

15. **Encouraging Worldwide Joint effort:**

In an interconnected world, the Lok Sabha perceives the significance of worldwide joint effort in tending to transnational wrongdoings and worldwide security challenges. Taking part in cooperative endeavors with global policing, taking part in joint tasks, and sharing prescribed procedures add to India's capacity to answer really to cross-line dangers. The Lok Sabha's help for worldwide joint effort highlights its obligation to an aggregate and worldwide way to deal with policing and security.

5.2 Training programs, equipment upgrades, and recruitment reforms

Preparing programs, gear updates, and enlistment changes are primary points of support in fortifying policing, upgrading their capacities, and guaranteeing they stay compelling in tending to the complicated difficulties of contemporary society. This extensive conversation digs into the multi-layered drives embraced by the Lok Sabha to put resources into preparing, modernize hardware, and change enlistment processes, underlining the basic job these components play in forming an expert and capable police force.

1. **Preparing Projects:**

Extensive Ability Improvement:

The Lok Sabha perceives that a thoroughly prepared police force is basic to successful policing. Drives zeroing in on complete expertise improvement structure a foundation of the preparation programs embraced by the Lok Sabha. These projects envelop an expansive range of abilities, including swarm the board, emergency exchange, criminological procedures, de-heightening strategies, local area commitment, and the moral utilization of power. The accentuation on a different range of abilities mirrors a comprehension that cutting edge policing expects officials to explore a large number of situations with accuracy and incredible skill.

Ceaseless Learning and Versatility:

The Lok Sabha advocates for a culture of ceaseless advancing inside policing. Perceiving the unique idea of wrongdoing and cultural difficulties, preparing programs are intended to be versatile and responsive.

Officials are given continuous open doors for proficient turn of events, guaranteeing that they keep up to date with arising patterns, mechanical progressions, and best practices in policing. The Lok Sabha's obligation to constant learning mirrors a comprehension that a thoroughly prepared and versatile police force is better prepared to address developing dangers.

Innovation Joining Preparing:

In accordance with the Lok Sabha's obligation to modernization, preparing programs are custom fitted to coordinate the most recent advancements into policing. Officials get preparing in the utilization of state of the art devices, for example, information examination, computerized reasoning, and advanced criminology. This guarantees that policing are capable in customary analytical strategies as well as prepared to saddle the force of innovation to upgrade their capacities. The Lok Sabha's accentuation on innovation coordination preparing lines up with the vision of making an innovatively proficient and forward-looking police force.

Specific Preparation Units:

Perceiving the requirement for particular ability to address explicit difficulties, the Lok Sabha upholds the production of specific preparation units inside policing. These units center around regions like cybercrime, counter-illegal intimidation, opiates authorization, and local area policing. By putting resources into particular preparation, the Lok Sabha guarantees that policing have the mastery expected to handle perplexing and concentrated crimes. This approach lines up with the contemporary requests put on police powers to address a different scope of dangers.

2. **Gear Overhauls:**

Modernizing Correspondence Frameworks:

Viable correspondence is fundamental for the coordination and reaction abilities of policing. The Lok Sabha advocates for the modernization of correspondence frameworks, guaranteeing that police staff approach cutting edge radio frameworks, encoded informing stages, and constant specialized instruments. Overhauling correspondence framework upgrades the productivity of reaction endeavors, works with between organization coordination, and adds to a more responsive and associated policing.

High level Scientific Innovation:

Putting resources into cutting edge criminological innovation is a critical focal point of hardware updates supported by the Lok Sabha. Criminological research facilities are outfitted with state of the art instruments for DNA investigation, finger impression recognizable proof, ballistics, and other measurable assessments. The combination of cutting edge criminological innovation speeds up the analytical cycle as well as guarantees the precision and dependability of proof introduced in court. The Lok Sabha's obligation to overhauling measurable capacities lines up determined to encourage a logical and proof based way to deal with criminal examinations.

Observation and Checking Apparatuses:

In light of the advancing idea of crimes, the Lok Sabha upholds the procurement of complex reconnaissance and checking devices. Shut circuit TV (CCTV) cameras, facial acknowledgment innovation, and high level observing frameworks add to upgrading the proactive abilities of policing. These devices help in wrongdoing counteraction, swarm observing, and the distinguishing proof of suspects, lining up with the Lok Sabha's vision of utilizing innovation to establish a more secure and safer climate.

Advanced Proof Administration Frameworks:

The Lok Sabha perceives the developing significance of advanced proof in criminal examinations. Drives incorporate the execution of hearty computerized proof administration frameworks, guaranteeing the solid stockpiling, recovery, and examination of electronic proof. Modernizing the treatment of computerized proof improves the productivity of examinations in a period where innovation assumes a focal part in crimes. The Lok Sabha's obligation to computerized proof administration mirrors a ground breaking way to deal with adjusting to the computerized age.

Defensive Stuff and Strategic Hardware:

Guaranteeing the security and prosperity of police faculty is a main concern for the Lok Sabha. Drives incorporate the arrangement of excellent defensive stuff and strategic hardware. Body reinforcement, revolt gear, and high level weaponry are given to upgrade the capacities of officials in answering testing and high-risk circumstances. The interest in defensive stuff defends the existences of police work force as well as imparts certainty and readiness in their capacity to actually satisfy their obligations.

3. **Enlistment Changes:**

Straightforward and Legitimacy Based Enlistment:

The Lok Sabha perceives the meaning of enlistment processes in forming the quality and impressive skill of policing. Drives incorporate changes pointed toward guaranteeing straightforward and merit-based enrollment. The Lok Sabha advocates for enrollment processes that are liberated from nepotism, bias, and defilement, guaranteeing that people are chosen in light of their capabilities, abilities, and reasonableness for policing. Straightforward enrollment processes add to building an able and different pool of competitors inside the police force.

Variety and Orientation Responsiveness:

Tending to the requirement for variety inside policing, Lok Sabha upholds enrollment changes to upgrade inclusivity. Drives incorporate endeavors to select people from assorted foundations, nationalities, and networks.

Furthermore, there is an emphasis on expanding the portrayal of ladies inside the police force. Orientation delicate enlistment practices and impetuses are acquainted with urge more ladies to seek after vocations in policing. The Lok Sabha's obligation to variety lines up with the rule that a police force intelligent of the more extensive populace is better prepared to address the requirements of different networks.

Tough Record verifications and Screening:

To guarantee the respectability and incredible skill of the police force, the Lok Sabha advocates for severe historical verifications and screening processes during enrollment. Intensive screening of up-and-comers, including checks for criminal history, monetary respectability, and moral guidelines, recognizes people with the most elevated levels of honesty and reasonableness for policing. Rigid screening processes add to building public trust and trust in the moral lead of the police force.

Complete Preparation for Volunteers:

Enlistment changes embraced by the Lok Sabha remember a concentration for extensive preparation for initiates. Recently enrolled officials go through thorough preparation programs that cover a scope of fundamental abilities, legitimate information, and moral contemplations. Preparing for initiates is intended to impart a feeling of obligation, obligation, and adherence to proficient norms from the start of their vocations. The Lok Sabha's obligation to vigorous preparation for initiates adds to building an underpinning of incredible skill and moral lead inside the police force.

Advancement of Local area Commitment:

Perceiving the significance of local area commitment in compelling policing, the Lok Sabha upholds enrollment changes that focus on people serious areas of strength for with abilities and a guarantee to local area administration. Drives incorporate evaluating competitors' capacity to connect decidedly with assorted networks, convey actually, and construct trust. By putting significance on local area commitment during enlistment, the Lok Sabha guarantees that officials are gifted in policing as well as have the characteristics vital for encouraging positive associations with the general population.

Utilization of Innovation in Enlistment:

In arrangement with the more extensive mechanical headways upheld by the Lok Sabha, enrollment processes are modernized using innovation. Online application frameworks, computerized appraisals, and information investigation are integrated to smooth out enlistment strategies, making them more proficient and open. Utilizing innovation in enlistment guarantees a fair and normalized process, adding to the general straightforwardness and viability of policing.

5.3 Showcasing improved outcomes due to these initiatives

The complete drives embraced by the Lok Sabha in the domains of preparing programs, hardware redesigns, and enrollment changes extraordinarily affect policing in India. These drives, altogether pointed toward upgrading the capacities, impressive skill, and responsiveness of the police force, have introduced superior results across different components of policing. This conversation digs into the positive changes and further developed results saw as an immediate consequence of the proactive measures carried out by the Lok Sabha.

1. **Improved Incredible skill and Ability:**

   The accentuation on exhaustive preparation programs has contributed altogether to the upgraded incredible skill and ability of the police force. Officials, furnished with different ranges of abilities and cutting-edge information, show a more significant level of capability in taking care of perplexing circumstances. The preparation drives supported by the Lok Sabha have imparted a feeling of certainty and versatility in policing, empowering them to explore many situations with more prominent viability. This elevated impressive skill converts into worked on open help, as officials are better prepared to maintain law and order and address the different difficulties they experience.

2. **Expanded Innovative Capability:**

   The reconciliation of trend setting innovation into policing, as supported by the Lok Sabha, has brought about a perceptible expansion in mechanical capability among police work force. Officials proficiently use state of the art apparatuses, for example, information examination, computerized reasoning, and advanced legal sciences in their analytical cycles. The utilization of current correspondence frameworks, observation devices, and advanced proof administration frameworks has smoothed out tasks, prompting faster and more precise reactions to crimes. The expanded mechanical capability lines up with the Lok Sabha's vision of an innovatively progressed police force fit for utilizing development to improve in general proficiency.

3. **Further developed Wrongdoing Anticipation and Discovery:**

   The modernization of hardware, including the organization of cutting edge observation devices and correspondence frameworks, has added to a perceptible improvement in wrongdoing counteraction and location. The utilization of CCTV cameras, facial acknowledgment innovation, and constant correspondence stages has upgraded the capacity of policing to quickly screen and answer crimes. Prescient policing, empowered by information examination, considers proactive measures in recognizing expected areas of interest and forestalling violations before they happen. Subsequently, there has been an unmistakable decrease in specific sorts of wrongdoings, and the police force is better situated to foresee and counter arising dangers.

4. **Proficient Treatment of Cybercrime:**

   The foundation and fortifying of particular units to address cybercrime, upheld by enrollment changes that focus on people with aptitude in computerized examinations, have prompted more effective treatment of digital related offenses. The police power's upgraded capacities in managing on the web misrepresentation, hacking, and computerized dangers are an immediate result of designated preparing programs and the sending of talented staff in cybercrime units. The proactive position in tending to digital dangers lines up with the Lok Sabha's obligation to remaining in front of developing difficulties in the advanced scene.

5. **Expanded Public Trust and Local area Relations:**

The attention on local area policing drives, directed by enlistment changes that underscore relational abilities and local area commitment, has brought about expanded public trust and further developed local area relations. Police work force, prepared to connect decidedly with different networks, effectively partake in local area outreach programs and team up with neighborhood associations. This approach cultivates a feeling of organization between the police and the general population, prompting more noteworthy collaboration in wrongdoing counteraction and detailing. As a result, the police force turns into an indispensable piece of the local area, working cooperatively to address nearby worries and construct a more secure climate.

6. **Quick and Viable Crisis Reaction:**

The modernization of correspondence frameworks and gear redesigns has converted into a more quick and successful crisis reaction from policing. Continuous specialized devices empower officials to facilitate consistently during emergency circumstances, further developing the general reaction time. The utilization of cutting edge scientific innovation helps with the quick assortment and examination of proof, working with the goal of cases all the more effectively. This straightforwardly affects public security, as policing can answer quickly to crises, relieve likely dangers, and give convenient help with basic circumstances.

7. **Decrease in Police Offense and Defilement:**

The Lok Sabha's obligation to enlistment changes, including rigid historical verifications and screening processes, has added to a decrease in occasions of police wrongdoing and debasement. By guaranteeing that enrollment processes are straightforward, merit-based, and liberated from bias, the police force is populated with people of high honesty. This significantly affects the in general moral direct of the power, encouraging a culture of responsibility and impressive skill. Severe historical verifications go about as an impediment to unfortunate behavior, prompting worked on open discernment and confidence in the moral principles of policing.

8. **Positive Effect on Wrongdoing Leeway Rates:**

The coordination of cutting edge innovation, combined with the accentuation on preparing programs, decidedly affects wrongdoing freedom rates. With upgraded insightful capacities, including the utilization of information investigation, computerized reasoning, and advanced legal sciences, policing can address cases all the more effectively. The superior treatment of proof, present day criminological methods, and particular preparation add to higher leeway rates across different sorts of wrongdoings. This not just reinforces the validity of the police force yet in addition goes about as an obstruction to crimes.

9. **Orientation Awareness and Local area Policing:**

Enrollment changes that focus on variety, remembering expanded portrayal of individuals for the police force, have prompted more noteworthy orientation responsiveness and further developed local area policing. Ladies officials, prepared in local area commitment and compromise, carry a remarkable point of view to policing. Their presence adds to a more comprehensive methodology in tending to the necessities of different networks. The enlistment of ladies officials emphatically affects the police power's picture, advancing a culture of correspondence and variety inside the association.

10. **Positive Effect on Official Prosperity:**

The accentuation on the prosperity of police faculty, through enlistment changes and extensive preparation programs, emphatically affects the psychological wellness and generally speaking prosperity of officials. Drives, for example, psychological well-being support programs, stress the executives assets, and further developed working circumstances add to a better and stronger labor force. This, thus, has an immediate connection with work fulfillment, diminished burnout, and expanded resolve inside the police force. A better and spurred labor force is better prepared to convey effective and merciful policing.

11. **Worldwide Acknowledgment and Cooperation:**

The drives attempted by the Lok Sabha in upgrading policing have earned worldwide acknowledgment and worked with global joint effort. The reception of current innovation, adherence to proficient norms, and support in joint tasks have situated Indian policing as important accomplices in the worldwide security scene. The positive results accomplished locally add to India's remaining in worldwide policing, encouraging coordinated effort with different countries in tending to transnational wrongdoings and worldwide security challenges.

12. **Improved Lawful Strengthening:**

The Lok Sabha's commitment with legitimate changes, including updates to existing regulation and the strengthening of policing with the essential lawful devices, has brought about a more engaged and certain police force. Clear and forward-thinking legitimate systems empower officials to complete their obligations with conviction, guaranteeing a harmony between successful policing insurance of individual privileges. The upgraded lawful strengthening adds to a more genuine and definitive police force, building up open confidence in the equity framework.

13. **Public Security and Insights:**

The positive results got from the Lok Sabha's drives have added to a general improvement in open security and view of policing. Quick and successful crisis reactions, local area commitment, decreased occasions of unfortunate behavior, and upgraded wrongdoing leeway rates add to a more secure climate for the general population. The positive collaborations between policing networks cultivate a conviction that all is good and participation. Subsequently, public view of policing have seen a positive shift, with expanded trust in their capacity to guarantee public wellbeing and maintain law and order.

Chapter 6

Improving Judicial Efficiency

Further developing legal proficiency is a complex test that requires extensive changes to upgrade the viability, openness, and responsiveness of the legal framework. The intricacies and excesses inside the overall set of laws can block the ideal goal of cases, influencing the conveyance of equity. This conversation investigates the drives, procedures, and changes embraced to work on legal productivity in India, zeroing in on the actions acquainted by the Lok Sabha with address these difficulties.

1. **Case The executives and Innovation Joining:**

   One of the key drives supported by the Lok Sabha to further develop legal proficiency is the execution of vigorous case the executives frameworks and the joining of innovation into the legal interaction. Customarily, paper-based cycles and manual record-keeping have added to deferrals and shortcomings. The presentation of case the board frameworks, upheld by advanced stages, has smoothed out case work processes, further developed record the executives, and worked with better correspondence among partners.

   The Lok Sabha's obligation to innovation reconciliation goes past essential case the executives. The reception of e-documenting frameworks, virtual court procedures, and electronic proof accommodation has reformed how cases are dealt with. This shift toward a computerized biological system facilitates case handling as well as upgrades straightforwardness and openness, permitting disputants, legal counselors, and judges to get to case-related data all the more effectively.

2. **Particular Courts and Case Task:**

   Perceiving the requirement for particular mastery in taking care of specific kinds of cases, the Lok Sabha has upheld the foundation of particular courts to address explicit legitimate areas. Specialization guarantees that judges directing specific cases have top to bottom information and involvement with the important lawful issues. This designated approach speeds up case goal and adds to a more compelling and concentrated legal executive.

Notwithstanding specialization, the Lok Sabha has accentuated the significance of key case task. Effective case portion guarantees that adjudicators with the imperative skill and experience handle explicit cases. This approach limits postpones brought about by an absence of knowledge of many-sided legitimate issues and adds to more powerful case the board.

3. **Elective Debate Goal (ADR):**

To reduce the weight on the conventional court framework, the Lok Sabha has effectively advanced the utilization of elective debate goal systems. ADR strategies, like intercession, discretion, and appeasement, offer prosecutors elective roads for settling debates outside the conventional court process. The Lok Sabha's support of ADR mirrors a pledge to lessening the excess of cases and furnishing disputants with quicker and more savvy choices for question goal.

The Lok Sabha's help for ADR is combined with drives to bring issues to light about these instruments and empower their use. This incorporates preparing programs for legitimate experts, mindfulness lobbies for people in general, and the foundation of ADR focuses. By establishing a climate helpful for ADR, the Lok Sabha adds to a more broadened and productive way to deal with compromise.

4. **Lawful Guide and Admittance to Equity:**

Guaranteeing admittance to equity for all residents is a crucial part of legal effectiveness. The Lok Sabha perceives the significance of lawful guide administrations, especially for helpless and minimized populaces who might confront obstructions in getting to the legal framework. Drives to upgrade legitimate guide administrations, including the development of lawful guide facilities and the arrangement of free administrations, add to a more comprehensive and open equity framework.

The Lok Sabha's obligation to legitimate guide is lined up with the rule that equivalent admittance to equity is fundamental for a fair and successful overall set of laws. By eliminating monetary hindrances and offering help to the people who can't bear the cost of lawful portrayal, the Lok Sabha adds to a more fair legal cycle.

5. **Legal Foundation and Asset Designation:**

A basic part of further developing legal proficiency is guaranteeing that the legal executive has the vital framework and assets to successfully work. The Lok Sabha has embraced drives to improve legal foundation, including the development of new court buildings, the arrangement of current offices, and the utilization of innovation to overhaul courts. These ventures add to a more favorable climate for case procedures, empowering judges and court staff to productively play out their obligations more.

Notwithstanding actual foundation, the Lok Sabha perceives the significance of key asset portion. Sufficient subsidizing for the legal executive guarantees that courts have the faculty, innovation, and backing administrations expected to immediately deal with cases. The Lok Sabha's obligation to asset portion lines up fully intent on building a legal executive that can really address the volume and intricacy of cases.

6. **Legal Preparation and Proceeding with Training:**

Perceiving the unique idea of the legitimate scene, the Lok Sabha has focused on legal preparation and proceeding with instruction programs. Judges are furnished with chances to upgrade their abilities, remain refreshed on legitimate turns of events, and find out about arising areas of regulation. These preparation programs add to the expert improvement of judges, guaranteeing that they are exceptional to deal with different and complex cases.

Legal preparation additionally stretches out to the utilization of innovation in legal actions. As a feature of the Lok Sabha's drives, judges get preparing on computerized stages, e-documenting frameworks, and virtual court procedures. This innovative proficiency enables judges to use present day apparatuses for case the executives, adding to more smoothed out and proficient court processes.

7. **Lessening Procedural Deferrals:**

Procedural deferrals have for some time been a test in the Indian legal framework. The Lok Sabha has effectively sought after changes to address these postponements and smooth out lawful systems. Drives incorporate the disentanglement of authoritative documents, the presentation of courses of events for case removal, and the decrease of pointless deferments. These actions mean to speed up the legal interaction and limit postpones brought about by procedural intricacies.

The Lok Sabha's attention on lessening procedural deferrals additionally stretches out to the presentation of case-stream the executives strategies. By executing case-stream the board techniques, courts can focus on cases in view of variables like intricacy, criticalness, and the accessibility of gatherings. This designated approach adds to more productive case goal and helps address the overabundance of cases.

8. **Legal Straightforwardness and Responsibility:**

Upgrading legal straightforwardness and responsibility is basic to building public confidence in the general set of laws. The Lok Sabha has upheld drives to advance straightforwardness in legal actions, including the live spilling of court procedures, the distribution of decisions on the web, and the arrangement of case-related data to people in general. These actions add to a more open and open legal executive, cultivating more prominent public trust in the lawful cycle.

Notwithstanding straightforwardness, the Lok Sabha perceives the significance of legal responsibility. Drives incorporate the foundation of systems for legal execution assessment, moral principles for judges, and the treatment of grievances against legal officials. By advancing responsibility, the Lok Sabha adds to a legal executive that works with honesty and is receptive to the assumptions for the general population.

9. **Lawful Changes and Administrative Changes:**

Lawful changes and regulative changes assume a crucial part in working on legal productivity. The Lok Sabha effectively takes part in authoritative drives to refresh and modernize existing regulations, address holes in the lawful system, and present procedural changes. This obligation to lawful changes lines up with the developing necessities of society and guarantees that the overall set of laws stays important and viable.

The Lok Sabha's commitment with lawful changes likewise reaches out to resolving issues like the build-up of cases, procedural intricacies, and the requirement for specific legitimate structures. By ordering regulations that answer contemporary difficulties, the Lok Sabha adds to an overall set of laws that is versatile, fair, and fit for conveying equity promptly.

10. **Public Mindfulness and Lawful Proficiency:**

Further developing legal productivity isn't exclusively the obligation of the overall set of laws; it likewise includes making mindfulness and advancing legitimate education among the overall population. The Lok Sabha upholds drives pointed toward upgrading public attention to lawful privileges, techniques, and the working of the legal framework. Lawful proficiency crusades, outreach programs, and instructive drives add to a more educated populace that can explore the legitimate cycle with more noteworthy comprehension.

Public mindfulness additionally stretches out to advancing the utilization of elective question goal instruments. The Lok Sabha's drives in such manner include spreading data about the advantages of intervention, assertion, and other ADR techniques.

By empowering disputants to investigate elective roads for debate goal, the Lok Sabha adds to the general decrease of caseloads in conventional courts.

11. **Legal Coordinated effort and Trade of Best Practices:**

The Lok Sabha perceives the worth of coordinated effort and the trading of best practices among various purviews. Drives incorporate working with legal gatherings, classes, and global coordinated efforts that permit judges to share bits of knowledge, encounters, and successful procedures for case the executives.

Gaining from fruitful practices carried out in different locales adds to the consistent improvement of the Indian legal framework.

Worldwide coordinated efforts likewise empower Indian adjudicators to remain refreshed on worldwide legitimate turns of events and developments. By cultivating a culture of joint effort, the Lok Sabha guarantees that the Indian legal executive remaining parts associated with worldwide prescribed procedures, adding to the continuous development and improvement of the overall set of laws.

6.1 Examination of Lok Sabha's measures to address the backlog of cases

The build-up of cases in the Indian legal framework has been a longstanding test that compromises the opportune conveyance of equity. The Lok Sabha, perceiving the direness of resolving this issue, has carried out a progression of measures and changes pointed toward handling the excess of cases. This assessment dives into the drives attempted by the Lok Sabha to lighten the weight of forthcoming cases and speed up the goal of legitimate questions.

1. **Case The executives Changes:**

   One of the focal mainstays of the Lok Sabha's methodology to address the accumulation of cases is the execution of case the board changes. The conventional way to deal with case the executives, described by paper-based cycles and manual record-keeping, frequently added to postponements and failures. The Lok Sabha, in arrangement with the standards of legal effectiveness, has advocated the reception of present day case the executives frameworks.

   These frameworks, controlled by innovation, empower the effective following and checking of cases from inception to goal. Computerized stages and e-documenting components have supplanted lumbering paper processes, smoothing out the progression of data inside the legal framework. Judges, legal counselors, and disputants can get to case-related data expeditiously, adding to a more straightforward and responsive legal interaction.

   Moreover, the Lok Sabha's underwriting of case the board changes incorporates the presentation of timetables for case removal.

   By laying out clear cutoff times for various phases of the judicial actions, the Lok Sabha plans to forestall pointless postponements and assist the goal of cases. This proactive way to deal with case the board lines up with the more extensive objective of making a more productive and responsible legal executive.

2. **Particular Courts for Facilitated Removal:**

   Perceiving that particular kinds of cases require specific ability, the Lok Sabha has upheld for the foundation of specific courts to facilitate the removal of cases falling inside unambiguous lawful areas. These specific courts, committed to dealing with specific classifications of cases, for example, business debates, family matters, or ecological issues, take into consideration a more engaged and effective settlement process.

The Lok Sabha's help for particular courts is twofold. To begin with, it guarantees that judges directing these specific courts have the fundamental information and involvement with the pertinent lawful regions. Second, it works with the making of devoted assets and framework customized to the one of a kind prerequisites of every classification of cases. This designated approach adds to decreasing the accumulation by smoothing out the treatment of cases through specific ability.

3. **Quick Track Courts and Opportune Removal:**

With an end goal to address the overabundance of cases, the Lok Sabha has advocated the foundation of quick track courts to manage particular sorts of cases that require critical consideration. These courts are intended to facilitate the lawful cycle and focus on the fast goal of cases, especially those including deplorable violations, ladies' security, or cases that have been forthcoming for a lengthy period.

The Lok Sabha's underwriting of quick track courts lines up with the guideline of guaranteeing convenient equity, particularly in situations where deferred goal might bring about unjustifiable difficulty or disavowal of equity. By diverting assets and thoughtfulness regarding cases with squeezing needs, quick track courts assume a vital part in decreasing the general excess and improving the effectiveness of the legal framework.

4. **Elective Debate Goal (ADR) Components:**

The Lok Sabha's drives to address the overabundance of cases stretch out past conventional court procedures to the advancement of elective debate goal (ADR) instruments. ADR, which incorporates strategies like intercession, assertion, and pacification, furnishes prosecutors with elective roads for settling questions outside the conventional court process.

The Lok Sabha perceives the capability of ADR in lessening the weight on customary courts by offering speedier and more financially savvy strategies for question goal. Drives incorporate the foundation of intervention focuses, the preparation of go betweens, and missions to bring issues to light about the advantages of ADR.

By empowering gatherings to investigate these elective roads, the Lok Sabha adds to the decongestion of ordinary courts and the mitigation of the build-up.

5. **Lawful Changes to Work on Methods:**

Working on lawful strategies is a critical part of tending to the build-up of cases, and the Lok Sabha has effectively sought after legitimate changes to smooth out processes and lessen superfluous intricacies. Drives incorporate the disentanglement of authoritative documents, the presentation of normalized methods, and endeavors to limit procedural obstacles that might add to delays.

By taking on an easy to understand way to deal with legitimate cycles, the Lok Sabha intends to make the legal framework more open and safe for defendants. This disentanglement not just facilitates the documenting and handling of cases yet in addition adds to a more comprehensive general set of laws that obliges the different requirements of defendants.

6. **Enrollment of Extra Adjudicators:**

   The lack of legal labor has been a contributing variable to the excess of cases. The Lok Sabha has tended to this test by pushing for the enlistment of extra adjudicators to increase the limit of the legal executive. By expanding the quantity of judges at different levels of the legal order, the Lok Sabha looks to improve the general limit of the framework to deal with a bigger volume of cases.

   The enlistment of extra adjudicators is supplemented by measures to speed up the determination cycle and address opening instantly. The Lok Sabha's obligation to reinforcing the legal labor force mirrors a comprehension that HR are a basic part in tending to the build-up and guaranteeing the proficient working of the overall set of laws.

7. **Utilization of Innovation in Court Procedures:**

   The Lok Sabha perceives the extraordinary capability of innovation in assisting court procedures and has effectively upheld the combination of innovation into the legal cycle. Virtual court procedures, video conferencing, and the utilization of computerized stages for hearings have become fundamental parts of the Lok Sabha's endeavors to modernize the general set of laws.

   The reception of innovation works with far off procedures as well as lessens the requirement for actual appearances in court, limiting calculated difficulties and time imperatives. This mechanical joining lines up with the Lok Sabha's obligation to utilizing development to improve the productivity of court procedures and add to the decrease of the overabundance.

8. **Observing and Detailing Systems:**

   Tending to the accumulation of cases requires viable observing and detailing systems to follow progress, distinguish bottlenecks, and execute restorative measures. The Lok Sabha has embraced drives to lay out observing frameworks that give continuous information on case pendency, removal rates, and other key execution pointers.

   These observing instruments empower the legal executive and important specialists to survey the effect of changes, distinguish regions that require consideration, and carry out techniques to address arising difficulties. The Lok Sabha's obligation to straightforward and information driven administration adds to a more responsible and responsive way to deal with dealing with the build-up of cases.

9. **Public Mindfulness and Investment:**

The Lok Sabha perceives the job of public mindfulness and support in tending to the accumulation of cases. Drives incorporate mindfulness crusades, legitimate proficiency projects, and endeavors to teach people in general about their freedoms as well as certain limitations in the lawful cycle. By cultivating a more educated and drawn in populace, the Lok Sabha adds to an overall set of laws in which prosecutors are better prepared to explore methods and add to the proficient goal of cases.

Public interest likewise reaches out to drives like Lok Adalats, where debates are settled through a course of placation and settlement. These people group based debate goal discussions, supported by the Lok Sabha, give a stage to the quick goal of cases and add to the decrease of the general build-up.

10. **Strategy Changes and Official Changes:**

The Lok Sabha's obligation to addressing the overabundance of cases stretches out to strategy changes and regulative changes pointed toward making a more versatile and responsive legitimate system. The authorization of regulations that address procedural intricacies, present new components for case removal, and answer arising legitimate difficulties mirrors the Lok Sabha's proactive way to deal with administrative changes.

Strategy changes embraced by the Lok Sabha incorporate exhaustive audits of existing regulations, conferences with legitimate specialists, and commitment with partners to distinguish regions requiring administrative consideration. By keeping the lawful structure refreshed and receptive to contemporary requirements, the Lok Sabha adds to the general productivity of the legal framework.

11. **Limit Building and Preparing Projects:**

Building the limit of legal officials and court staff is a basic part of tending to the excess of cases. The Lok Sabha upholds preparing programs pointed toward improving the abilities of judges, court agents, and other work force associated with the legal interaction.

These projects cover regions like case the executives, legitimate exploration, and the utilization of innovation in court procedures.

Limit building drives are intended to enable legal officials to deal with cases all the more productively, take on prescribed procedures, and remain refreshed on legitimate turns of events. By putting resources into the expert improvement of the legal executive, the Lok Sabha adds to a more proficient and versatile overall set of laws that can successfully address the difficulties presented by the overabundance.

12. **Legal Joint effort and Trade of Best Practices:**

Perceiving the significance of cooperation among various wards, the Lok Sabha empowers legal coordinated effort and the trading of best practices. Drives incorporate legal meetings, courses, and gatherings that furnish decided with chances to share bits of knowledge, encounters, and viable systems for case the executives.

Global coordinated efforts are likewise worked with to empower Indian appointed authorities to gain from effective practices carried out in different nations. By encouraging a culture of cooperation, the Lok Sabha guarantees that the Indian legal executive remaining parts associated with worldwide prescribed procedures, adding to the continuous development and improvement of the general set of laws.

6.2 Introduction of alternative dispute resolution mechanisms

Elective Question Goal (ADR) components have arisen as fundamental parts of present day general sets of laws, offering parties engaged with debates an elective way to settling clashes outside the conventional court setting. The presentation and advancement of ADR components connote a change in perspective in the way to deal with question goal, underlining productivity, adaptability, and consensual goal over the ill-disposed nature of suit. This investigation dives into the idea of ADR, its importance with regards to contemporary general sets of laws, and the drives taken by different substances, including authoritative bodies like the Lok Sabha, to incorporate ADR into the more extensive structure of equity.

Figuring out Elective Debate Goal (ADR):

Elective Question Goal includes a scope of cycles and procedures pointed toward settling debates without turning to formal case. Dissimilar to conventional court procedures, which include an adjudicatory choice by an adjudicator or jury, ADR techniques focus on cooperative and consensual goals. The essential types of ADR incorporate intervention, discretion, mollification, exchange, and different half breed processes.

Intervention:

Intervention includes a nonpartisan outsider, known as a middle person, working with correspondence between questioning gatherings to assist them with arriving at a commonly satisfactory goal. The arbiter doesn't decide however helps the gatherings in recognizing shared view and creating their own answers.

Mediation:

Mediation is a semi legal cycle where an impartial judge or a board of mediators is enabled to settle on a limiting choice on the question. Discretion procedures frequently copy the construction of trials, yet they offer more noteworthy adaptability regarding methods and proof.

Appeasement:

Placation is like intercession, with an outsider conciliator helping parties in arriving at a settlement. Nonetheless, in placation, the conciliator might assume a more dynamic part in proposing arrangements and making proposals.

Exchange:

Exchange includes direct correspondence between the gatherings without the inclusion of an outsider. It is a casual interaction where the actual gatherings endeavor to arrive at a goal through exchange and split the difference.

Crossover Cycles:

Crossover processes consolidate components of various ADR techniques to suit the particular requirements of a question. For instance, "prescription arb" includes an underlying intervention stage, with discretion as a backup plan in the event that intercession neglects to deliver a goal.

Meaning of ADR in Contemporary General sets of laws:

The developing meaning of ADR in contemporary general sets of laws is attached in its capacity to address a few deficiencies related with customary suit. The reception and coordination of ADR components into legitimate structures, including regulative drives by substances like the Lok Sabha, mirror an acknowledgment of the accompanying key benefits:

Productivity and Practicality:

ADR processes are in many cases more speedy than conventional court procedures. Parties have more noteworthy command over the speed of the goal, and ADR can be organized to meet explicit timetables, adding to quicker debate goal.

Cost-Viability:

Customary case can be monetarily difficult because of legitimate charges, court costs, and different costs. ADR by and large includes lower costs as it is less formal and smoothed out, making it an appealing choice for parties looking for an additional efficient method for settling debates.

Adaptability and Customization:

ADR permits gatherings to fit the goal interaction to their interesting necessities and conditions. This adaptability is especially worthwhile in complex debates where a one-size-fits-all approach might be unreasonable.

Safeguarding of Connections:

Not at all like ill-disposed court processes, ADR advances a cooperative and helpful methodology. This can be critical in protecting connections, particularly in questions including continuous business connections, family matters, or local area issues.

Secrecy:

ADR processes frequently give a more significant level of classification contrasted with court procedures. This privacy supports open correspondence between parties, as they can uninhibitedly investigate expected arrangements unafraid of public exposure.

Strengthening of Gatherings:

ADR enables parties by giving them a functioning job in the goal cycle. In intercession and discussion, for example, parties have the valuable chance to straightforwardly partake in creating arrangements, encouraging a feeling of responsibility over the result.

Diminished Caseloads and Overabundances:

ADR can contribute altogether to lessening the caseloads and excesses in customary courts. By redirecting specific debates to ADR components, the burden on the court framework is eased, permitting it to zero in on cases that require settlement.

Social Responsiveness:

ADR cycles can be intended to oblige and regard different social standards and values. This makes ADR especially pertinent in multicultural social orders where various networks might favor goal techniques that line up with their social points of view.

Administrative Acknowledgment and Advancement of ADR:

The Lok Sabha, as the lower place of the Parliament of India, plays had a vital impact in perceiving the significance of ADR and consolidating regulative measures to advance its utilization. Regulative drives by the Lok Sabha mirror a forward-looking way to deal with debate goal, recognizing that the legitimate scene should adjust to developing cultural necessities. A portion of the vital regulative activities and drives include:

The Mediation and Pacification Act, 1996:

The Discretion and Placation Act, 1996, is a milestone regulation that oversees mediation and mollification procedures in India.

Established to line up with worldwide prescribed procedures, the Demonstration advances the utilization of intervention as a favored strategy for debate goal. It gives a lawful structure to the implementation of arbitral honors and blueprints the strategies for both homegrown and global discretion.

The Lok Sabha's support of the Discretion and Pacification Act mirrors a guarantee to establishing a helpful climate for elective question goal. The Demonstration urges gatherings to select intervention and placation as proficient and successful options in contrast to customary suit.

The Business Courts, Business Division, and Business Investigative Division of High Courts Act, 2015:

The Business Courts Act, sanctioned in 2015, plans to facilitate the goal of business debates by laying out business courts at different levels. It envelops arrangements for pre-foundation intervention and settlement, stressing the job of ADR systems in settling business debates.

This administrative drive lines up with the Lok Sabha's obligation to advancing effectiveness in question goal, especially with regards to business matters. The consideration of pre-organization intercession as a required step highlights the acknowledgment of intervention as a significant instrument for settling questions before formal judicial procedures.

Public Lawful Administrations Authority (NALSA) Act, 1987:

The Public Legitimate Administrations Authority Act, established in 1987, is a regulative measure pointed toward giving free and skillful lawful administrations to the more vulnerable segments of society. It laid out the Public Lawful Administrations Authority (NALSA) to work with admittance to equity for underestimated networks.

While not solely centered around ADR, the NALSA Act underscores the significance of lawful guide and elective debate goal systems in guaranteeing equivalent admittance to equity. The Lok Sabha's help for this regulation mirrors a promise to making equity open to all fragments of society.

The Buyer Security Act, 2019:

The Buyer Security Act, 2019, acquainted huge changes with purchaser assurance regulations in India. The regulation incorporates arrangements for the foundation of intercession cells at the area, state, and public levels to work with the goal of purchaser debates through intervention.

By consolidating intervention as a focal component in the goal of buyer debates, the Lok Sabha perceives the capability of ADR in resolving issues that frequently include customers and organizations. The accentuation on intervention lines up with the more extensive objective of giving quick and financially savvy answers for purchaser complaints.

Drives to Advance ADR Past Regulation:

Past administrative measures, the Lok Sabha has effectively upheld drives to advance ADR through mindfulness crusades, preparing projects, and coordinated efforts with partners. These drives mirror a complete way to deal with cultivating a culture of elective debate goal in the legitimate scene:

Mindfulness Missions and Effort:

The Lok Sabha has been instrumental in supporting mindfulness missions to teach the general population, legitimate experts, and organizations about the advantages of ADR. These missions intend to dissipate legends encompassing ADR, feature its benefits, and urge gatherings to think about elective strategies for question goal.

By cultivating a superior comprehension of ADR, the Lok Sabha adds to establishing a legitimate climate where gatherings are more open to investigating elective roads for settling debates.

Preparing and Limit Building:

Perceiving the requirement for talented experts in the field of ADR, the Lok Sabha has supported preparing and limit building programs. These projects target judges, legal counselors, arbiters, and different partners associated with the debate goal process.

The Lok Sabha's help for preparing drives mirrors a comprehension that the progress of ADR relies upon the capability and skill of those working with the goal interaction. Preparing programs add to the improvement of a talented framework of ADR specialists.

Consolidating ADR in Lawful Training:

The Lok Sabha perceives the significance of incorporating ADR standards into lawful schooling. By stressing ADR in graduate school educational programs, future legitimate experts are presented to the different components accessible for settling debates, setting them up for a lawful scene that values options in contrast to conventional case.

This drive adds to a social shift inside the legitimate local area, empowering a proactive and educated way to deal with the utilization regarding ADR by and by.

Joint efforts and Associations:

The Lok Sabha has worked with joint efforts and associations with associations and elements associated with the ADR space. These joint efforts might include the trading of best practices, the foundation of intervention focuses, and the improvement of systems to upgrade the adequacy of ADR components.

By encouraging coordinated efforts, the Lok Sabha guarantees that the advancement of ADR is an aggregate exertion that draws on the skill and assets of different partners.

Difficulties and Contemplations:

While the advancement of ADR by the Lok Sabha and different substances denotes a positive move toward a more enhanced and proficient equity framework, certain difficulties and contemplations should be tended to:

Social Discernments:

Conventional perspectives on equity and debate goal might represent a test to the inescapable acknowledgment of ADR. Social insights that focus on antagonistic case as the essential strategy for settling debates might should be tended to through designated mindfulness crusades.

Asset Assignment:

Satisfactory assets, including prepared go betweens and authorities, are fundamental for the compelling execution of ADR components. The Lok Sabha's obligation to ADR ought to be joined by asset portion measures to guarantee the accessibility of talented experts and foundation.

Requirement of ADR Grants:

The requirement of ADR grants is a basic part of the viability of these components. The Lok Sabha, through administrative measures, ought to address any difficulties connected with the requirement of arbitral honors and intervened settlements, guaranteeing that the results of ADR processes are regarded and maintained.

Institutional Structures:

The foundation and reinforcing of institutional structures for ADR are significant for its prosperity. The Lok Sabha's drives ought to zero in on making hearty establishments, for example, intercession focuses and discretion bodies, to help the development and manageability of ADR.

Joining with Legal Cycles:

The Lok Sabha's underwriting of ADR ought to be supplemented by endeavors to flawlessly incorporate ADR with customary legal cycles. Clear rules and instruments for alluding cases to ADR, guaranteeing similarity with court procedures, and advancing a cooperative connection between ADR specialists and the legal executive are fundamental.

6.3 Success stories of improved judicial efficiency in specific regions

Endeavors to upgrade legal proficiency have yielded examples of overcoming adversity in different locales all over the planet, where creative practices and changes have prompted better case the board, diminished excess, and smoothed out court processes.

These examples of overcoming adversity highlight the extraordinary effect of designated mediations in the overall set of laws. This investigation features a few striking instances of districts that have seen positive results with regards to legal effectiveness.

1. **Singapore:**

   Singapore has acquired worldwide acknowledgment for its obligation to legal greatness and productivity. The city-state has carried out a scope of drives to improve its general set of laws, zeroing in on utilizing innovation, particular courts, and case the board changes.

   Electronic Recording and Case The board:

   Singapore's reception of electronic documenting and case the board frameworks has fundamentally sped up court processes. The utilization of innovation takes into consideration consistent recording of reports, effective case following, and electronic correspondence among partners. This has decreased regulatory postponements, improved openness to case data, and added to a more straightforward overall set of laws.

   Specific Business Courts:

   Perceiving the significance of specific mastery in settling complex business questions, Singapore laid out the Singapore Global Business Court (SICC). The SICC contains experienced global and neighborhood judges, and its systems are intended to take care of the exceptional necessities of worldwide business cases. The making of specific courts like the SICC has prompted quicker goal of business questions and expanded Singapore's appeal as a worldwide legitimate center point.

   Case The executives Procedures:

   Singapore has embraced case the executives procedures to guarantee the productive movement of cases through the overall set of laws. The legal executive effectively participates in early case meetings, where judges, attorneys, and defendants examine case issues and investigate settlement prospects. This proactive methodology adds to the opportune demeanor of cases and diminishes the probability of extended suit.

2. **Joined Realm:**

The Assembled Realm has gone through critical changes pointed toward working on the effectiveness of its legal framework. These changes envelop changes in court processes, reception of innovation, and drives to address overabundance issues.

Online Court Framework:

The presentation of a web-based court framework in the UK has upset how certain cases are dealt with. The Web-based Court, at first executed for low-esteem common cases, permits disputants to document cases, submit proof, and partake in hearings on the web. This diminishes the weight on conventional courts as well as gives a more open and easy to understand stage for question goal.

Brought together Family Court Framework:

To smooth out family regulation cases and guarantee a more all encompassing methodology, the UK has executed a Bound together Family Court framework. This incorporated framework solidifies family regulation matters under a solitary court, diminishing the requirement for different court appearances and improving on case the board. The Bound together Family Court improves the effectiveness of dealing with family questions and guarantees an organized way to deal with related issues.

Legal Case The executives:

Legal case the executives rehearses have been reinforced to address accumulation concerns. Passes judgment on assume a more dynamic part in overseeing cases, setting clear schedules, and effectively captivating with gatherings to support settlements. Case the board strategies, for example, the utilization of pre-preliminary survey hearings, guarantee that cases are satisfactorily ready prior to arriving at preliminary, adding to faster and more productive goals.

3. **US:**

In the US, different states have executed creative measures to upgrade legal proficiency, consolidating innovation, specific courts, and elective question goal components.

E-Recording Frameworks:

Numerous U.S. states have taken on electronic documenting frameworks to modernize court systems. E-recording permits lawyers and prosecutors to submit archives electronically, lessening administrative work, speeding up documenting processes, and improving the general productivity of the court framework. States, for example, Texas and California have effectively carried out far reaching e-recording frameworks.

Business Courts and Business Agendas:

Perceiving the requirement for specific mastery in dealing with complex business questions, a few U.S. wards have laid out business courts or business agendas. These specific courts, frequently set up by decided with mastery in business and business regulation, work with the quick goal of perplexing business cases. Delaware, known for its Court of Chancery, is a striking model where business debates are settled effectively, adding to the state's conspicuousness in corporate regulation.

Critical thinking Courts:

The U.S. has seen the rise of critical thinking courts, including drug courts, psychological wellness courts, and veterans' courts. These specific courts center around resolving the hidden issues adding to particular kinds of cases, for example, substance misuse or emotional wellness issues. By giving designated mediations and recovery programs, critical thinking courts mean to diminish recidivism and mitigate the weight on customary crook courts.

4. **Canada:**

Canada has embraced drives to further develop admittance to equity, decrease postponements, and upgrade the productivity of its overall set of laws. Different areas have executed changes to address explicit difficulties and modernize court processes.

Case The executives and Early Goal:

Regions like Ontario have embraced case the board practices to work with early goal and effective case movement. Case the executives includes early legal intercession to set courses of events, distinguish issues, and empower settlement conversations. This proactive methodology has added to the ideal goal of cases and a decrease in excess.

Utilization of Innovation in Far off Hearings:

The reception of innovation for far off hearings, particularly during the Coronavirus pandemic, plays had a significant impact in keeping up with court tasks. Video conferencing and virtual hearings have become fundamental to the Canadian lawful scene, permitting procedures to go on while conquering geological boundaries. This has added to effectiveness as well as expanded availability to equity.

Incorporated Equity Frameworks:

A few territories in Canada have executed coordinated equity frameworks that associate different parts of the equity framework, including courts, police, and legitimate administrations. These frameworks smooth out data sharing, lessen duplication, and improve coordination among various elements. The joining of equity frameworks adds to a more strong and effective legitimate system.

5. **Australia:**

Australia has carried out changes pointed toward working on the proficiency of its overall set of laws, with an emphasis on case the executives, innovation reception, and elective question goal.

Case The executives Changes:

Australian purviews have acquainted case the board changes with speed up the goal of cases. Case the board includes dynamic legal oversight, early ID of issues, and setting timetables for different phases of the lawful interaction. This approach has been especially successful in lessening delays and guaranteeing the ideal demeanor of cases.

Public ADR System:

Australia has embraced elective question goal as a vital piece of its legitimate scene. The Public ADR Structure advances the utilization of intervention and other ADR strategies to determine questions outside customary court procedures. Drives, for example, court-added intervention projects and preparing for legitimate experts add to the progress of ADR in Australia.

Innovation in Court Cycles:

The reception of innovation in court processes has been a critical concentration in Australia. E-documenting frameworks, online debate goal stages, and video conferencing for trials have been carried out to smooth out techniques and upgrade openness. These mechanical headways add to the productivity of the overall set of laws.

Chapter 7

Enhancing Access to Justice

Improving Admittance to Equity: An All encompassing Way to deal with Lawful Strengthening

Admittance to equity, a crucial principle of a fair and impartial society, epitomizes the possibility that all people ought to have the means and capacity to look for a cure through the general set of laws. Be that as it may, this entrance has frequently been obliged by different boundaries, including monetary, social, and institutional variables. Improving admittance to equity is a diverse test that requires a comprehensive methodology enveloping lawful changes, creative instruments, and a pledge to inclusivity. This investigation digs into the intricacies of admittance to equity, the hindrances looked by different populaces, and the techniques utilized universally to make a legitimate scene that is open, responsive, and engaging.

Grasping Admittance to Equity:

Admittance to equity isn't just a legitimate idea; it is a central basic freedom established in the standards of reasonableness, uniformity, and law and order. At its center, admittance to equity guarantees that people can look for legitimate cures, safeguard their freedoms, and take part seriously in the lawful cycle. This includes a scope of common, criminal, and managerial issues, underscoring the significance of a general set of laws that is congenial, justifiable, and accessible to all.

Financial Hindrances:

One of the essential hindrances to admittance to equity is monetary dissimilarity. Judicial actions frequently involve significant expenses, including legitimate charges, court charges, and other related costs. For people with restricted monetary assets, exploring the general set of laws turns into an overwhelming possibility. The powerlessness to manage the cost of legitimate portrayal or cover procedural expenses can bring about a huge difference in the capacity to get to equity.

Geological and Social Boundaries:

Geological and social elements add to variations in admittance to equity. Rustic people group might confront difficulties connected with the actual separation from lawful assets, making it challenging for inhabitants to get to legitimate administrations. Also, underestimated and weak populaces, including ethnic minorities and foreigners, may experience social boundaries like language hindrances, segregation, and absence of social capability inside the overall set of laws.

Intricacy of Legitimate Cycles:

The intricacy of legitimate strategies and documentation represents a significant obstruction to admittance to equity. Legitimate cycles are frequently perplexing, requiring a nuanced comprehension of the law and procedural complexities. People without legitimate mastery might find it trying to explore these intricacies, prompting an absence of trust in drawing in with the general set of laws.

Lacking Lawful Guide:

The accessibility and sufficiency of lawful guide administrations assume a vital part in guaranteeing admittance to equity for the people who can't manage the cost of private legitimate portrayal. Be that as it may, lacking financing, restricted extension, and qualification standards frequently confine the adequacy of lawful guide programs. This represents an obstruction to people who may not meet severe rules but rather still face lawful difficulties.

Mechanical Hindrances:

In the advanced period, the combination of innovation in lawful cycles can be a situation with two sides. While mechanical progressions can possibly upgrade proficiency, they may likewise make obstructions for people who need advanced education or admittance to online assets. Computerized partitions can compound variations in admittance to equity, especially for underestimated networks.

Worldwide Drives to Upgrade Admittance to Equity:

Perceiving the multi-layered nature of boundaries to get to equity, nations and global associations have carried out different drives to upgrade availability, inclusivity, and effectiveness inside overall sets of laws. These drives plan to address financial, geological, and social inconsistencies, guaranteeing that equity isn't an honor yet an ideal for all.

Legitimate Guide Changes:

Numerous purviews have gone through legitimate guide changes to grow the degree and adequacy of lawful help programs. This incorporates expanding subsidizing for legitimate guide associations, widening qualification rules, and coordinating local area based lawful administrations. Britain and Ridges, for example, have carried out changes to work on the quality and accessibility of lawful guide, guaranteeing that people with restricted monetary means can get to legitimate portrayal.

Local area Legitimate Strengthening:

Local area based legitimate strengthening programs engage people to comprehend and state their privileges inside their networks. Non-legislative associations (NGOs) and lawful guide suppliers team up to convey legitimate schooling, studios, and facilities in underserved regions. These drives upgrade lawful proficiency as well as construct a feeling of local area strength against bad form. In nations like Kenya, people group lawful strengthening programs have been fruitful in tending to nearby equity needs.

Free Lawful Administrations:

Free lawful administrations, gave willfully by legitimate experts, overcome any issues for people who can't bear the cost of private portrayal. Law offices and individual legal advisors contribute their skill to serve minimized networks and underrepresented gatherings. Drives like the American Bar Affiliation's Model Rule 6.1 urge legal counselors to commit a piece of their expert chance to free administrations, cultivating a culture of social obligation inside the legitimate calling.

Innovation for Legitimate Strengthening:

Outfitting innovation is an incredible asset for improving admittance to equity. Online legitimate assets, virtual lawful centers, and portable applications have arisen to give data, direction, and backing to people confronting lawful difficulties. In India, for instance, the Versatile Sahyogini application helps provincial ladies in understanding and getting to lawful cures connected with abusive behavior at home.

Court Improvement and Self improvement Administrations:

Courts in different purviews have executed drives to improve on legitimate cycles and give self improvement administrations. This incorporates plain-language court structures, online help devices, and court pilots to direct people through strategies. The California Courts' Self improvement Habitats, for example, offer assets and help to self-addressed disputants, meaning to demystify the overall set of laws and upgrade openness.

Elective Question Goal (ADR) Instruments:

ADR systems, including intercession and assertion, offer options in contrast to customary case, advancing speedier and more financially savvy debate goal.

By empowering gatherings to partake effectively in settling clashes, ADR mitigates boundaries related with the antagonistic idea of court procedures. The Australian Question Goal Warning Board (ADRAC) elevates ADR practices to upgrade admittance to equity in Australia.

Legitimate Tech New companies:

The ascent of legitimate tech new companies has acquainted creative arrangements with democratize admittance to lawful administrations. These new businesses influence man-made reasoning, online stages, and mechanization to give reasonable and easy to use legitimate help. Organizations like LegalZoom in the US and DoNotPay worldwide deal online devices that work on legitimate cycles and give direction to clients without lawful aptitude.

Difficulties and Contemplations:

Notwithstanding the headway made in upgrading admittance to equity, a few difficulties persevere, requiring progressing consideration and creative arrangements:

Maintainability of Lawful Guide Projects:

The manageability of legitimate guide programs stays a test, with numerous wards confronting spending plan requirements and asset constraints. Sufficient financing and long haul responsibilities are fundamental to guarantee the proceeded with adequacy of legitimate guide administrations.

Social and Semantic Awareness:

Accomplishing genuine admittance to equity requires social and semantic awareness inside overall sets of laws. Perceiving and tending to the assorted necessities of networks, including semantic minorities, native populaces, and socially particular gatherings, is urgent to conquering fundamental obstructions.

Advanced Incorporation:

The shift toward computerized stages for lawful administrations requires an emphasis on computerized consideration. Endeavors ought to be made to address the computerized partition by giving preparation, assets, and availability elements to guarantee that innovation doesn't make new boundaries for weak populaces.

Lawful Training and Proficiency:

Working on lawful training and proficiency is essential to enabling people to explore the general set of laws. Drives ought to zero in on coordinating lawful training into school educational plans, advancing local area based legitimate proficiency projects, and cultivating a comprehension of legitimate freedoms as well as certain limitations.

Cooperation Across Areas:

Compelling answers for improve admittance to equity require coordinated effort across areas, including government, legitimate experts, NGOs, and the confidential area. Building organizations and sharing assets can enhance the effect of drives, making a more firm and interconnected way to deal with equity.

Tending to Foundational Shameful acts:

Genuine admittance to equity includes tending to foundational treacheries and primary disparities. Legitimate changes shouldn't just zero in on procedural improvements yet in addition challenge oppressive practices, predispositions, and strategies that propagate disparities inside the general set of laws.

7.1 Initiatives to make the justice system more accessible to all citizens

Admittance to equity is a foundation of a fair and vote based society, guaranteeing that all residents possess the ability to look for change, safeguard their freedoms, and take part in legitimate cycles. In any case, various obstructions have generally restricted admittance, lopsidedly influencing underestimated and weak populaces.

Perceiving the basic to address these difficulties, legislatures, lawful establishments, and common society associations all over the planet have carried out a scope of drives to make the equity framework more open, fair, and comprehensive. This investigation digs into key drives pointed toward separating hindrances, enabling residents, and encouraging an equity framework that serves the requirements of different networks.

1. **Lawful Guide Changes:**

   One of the basic systems to improve admittance to equity includes exhaustive changes to lawful guide administrations. Lawful guide is a basic part in guaranteeing that people who can't bear the cost of private legitimate portrayal actually have significant admittance to the overall set of laws. Changes in this space envelop a few aspects:

   Expanded Financing: State run administrations and legitimate organizations have done whatever it takes to apportion more assets to lawful guide administrations. Sufficient financing guarantees the maintainability and viability of lawful guide programs, permitting them to arrive at a more extensive portion of the populace.

   Extended Qualification Models: Changes frequently include growing the qualification rules for legitimate guide to incorporate a more extensive scope of people. This incorporates changing pay limits, taking into account the intricacy of cases, and perceiving the particular necessities of weak gatherings.

   Local area Based Legitimate Guide: Drives to bring lawful guide benefits nearer to networks have built up some decent momentum. Local area based lawful guide centers, frequently show to non-administrative associations (NGOs) and legitimate experts, offer confined help, address local area explicit issues, and overcome any barrier between lawful administrations and residents.

2. **Free Legitimate Administrations:**

   The idea of free lawful administrations includes legitimate experts offering their mastery intentionally to people who can't manage the cost of lawful portrayal. Free drives contribute altogether to widening admittance to equity:

   Law office Responsibilities: Numerous law offices currently focus on free work as a feature of their corporate social obligation. They urge their lawful experts to devote a piece of their opportunity to offering free legitimate types of assistance to those out of luck, in this way growing the scope of legitimate help.

   Free Organizations: Cooperative organizations of lawful experts, NGOs, and local area associations cooperate to make free organizations. These organizations smooth out the matching system, interfacing attorneys with people or causes that need free legitimate help.

Worldwide Free Drives: Worldwide drives, like the Free Announcement for the Americas, unite lawful experts from different locales to focus on free work. These drives cultivate a culture of lawful obligation and coordinated effort on a more extensive scale.

3. **Innovation for Lawful Strengthening:**

In the computerized age, innovation has arisen as an amazing asset to democratize admittance to lawful administrations. Different drives influence innovation to defeat geological, monetary, and enlightening hindrances:

Online Lawful Assets: Stages giving free internet based legitimate assets, data, and self improvement instruments enable people to figure out legitimate cycles and explore the framework. Sites like Legitimate Guide Online in the UK and LawHelp.org in the US offer exhaustive lawful data to people in general.

Virtual Lawful Centers: The appearance of virtual legitimate facilities empowers people to remotely look for lawful exhortation and help. Through video conferencing, visit, or email, people can associate with legitimate experts without the requirement for actual presence, conquering geological limitations.

Portable Applications: Versatile applications intended to give lawful data and direction have acquired prominence. These applications take care of explicit legitimate necessities, like family regulation, occupant freedoms, or work regulation. For example, the My Lawful Mate application in Australia offers legitimate data customized to the necessities of youngsters.

4. **Local area Lawful Strengthening:**

Engaging people group to comprehend and declare their lawful freedoms is a significant part of making the equity framework more open. Local area legitimate strengthening drives include:

Legitimate Proficiency Projects: Projects that attention on lawful education intend to instruct networks about their freedoms as well as limitations. Studios, courses, and instructive materials are utilized to upgrade understanding and enable people to explore legitimate cycles.

Local area Lawful Instruction Habitats: Laying out local area legitimate training places carries lawful assets nearer to networks. These focuses give an actual space where people can get to data, look for direction, and take part in legitimate training programs.

Associations with NGOs: Joint efforts between lawful establishments and non-administrative associations upgrade local area legitimate strengthening. NGOs frequently assume a critical part in creating and carrying out programs that address explicit legitimate requirements inside networks.

5. **Elective Question Goal (ADR) Systems:**

Empowering the utilization of elective question goal systems, like intercession and discretion, furnishes residents with options in contrast to customary suit. ADR drives offer a few benefits regarding openness:

Intervention Administrations: Numerous purviews have laid out court-added intercession projects to urge gatherings to agreeably determine debates. Intervention administrations are in many cases given via prepared go betweens, offering a practical and opportune goal choice.

Local area Intervention Focuses: People group based intercession habitats work autonomously of formal court processes. These focuses, staffed via prepared local area middle people, take care of limited debates and add to encouraging a culture of goal inside networks.

Motivations for ADR: States and lawful establishments might acquaint impetuses for parties with choose ADR processes. These motivators could incorporate diminished court charges for cases that go through intercession or assisted courses of events for cases settled through discretion.

6. **Improvement of Lawful Cycles:**

The intricacy of legitimate cycles can go about as a huge obstruction to get to. Disentanglement drives mean to make legitimate systems more reasonable and traversable:

Plain-Language Court Structures: Growing plain-language court structures guarantees that people can without much of a stretch grasp and complete essential reports. This lessens disarray and engages people to take part actually in judicial procedures.

Online Help Devices: Online stages that give bit by bit direction and help with finishing authoritative archives improve on the cycle for people addressing themselves. Intelligent devices can upgrade procedural comprehension and guarantee that people meet necessities.

Court Pilots: Presenting court guides, people prepared to help self-addressed defendants, can direct people through the court interaction. This human help helps overcome any barrier for those new to lawful methodology.

7. **Reinforcing Legal Variety:**

Guaranteeing variety inside the legal executive is fundamental for building trust in the general set of laws and advancing a more comprehensive way to deal with equity:

Various Legal Arrangements: States can carry out approaches and practices that advance variety in legal arrangements. This includes effectively looking for applicants from underrepresented gatherings and guaranteeing that the legal executive mirrors the variety of the populace it serves.

Preparing on Social Capability: Giving preparation on social skill to passes judgment on guarantees a legal executive that is receptive to the special necessities of different networks. This preparing upgrades the capacity of judges to comprehend and address the social setting of lawful issues.

Local area Commitment by the Legal executive: Judges drawing in with networks through outreach programs, official Q&A events, and instructive drives add to building a more straightforward and receptive equity framework. This proactive commitment encourages a feeling of association between the legal executive and general society.

Difficulties and Contemplations:

While these drives address huge steps toward a more open equity framework, challenges persevere, requiring continuous consideration and refinement:

Guaranteeing Supportability: The drawn out maintainability of drives requires continuous responsibility from states, lawful foundations, and partners. Sufficient financing, predictable strategies, and occasional assessments are fundamental to support the effect of admittance to equity programs.

Adjusting to Mechanical Advances: As innovation develops, guaranteeing that drives remain innovatively important and open to different populaces is essential. Endeavors should be made to connect the advanced separation and address differences in computerized proficiency.

Tending to Fundamental Imbalances: Drives ought to be intended to address foundational disparities inside the general set of laws. This incorporates recognizing and effectively attempting to amend inclinations, segregation, and boundaries that may excessively influence specific networks.

Estimating Effect: Creating hearty instruments to quantify the effect of drives is fundamental for surveying their viability. Observing markers like expanded legitimate education, decreased caseloads, and further developed fulfillment among clients refines and improve programs.

Cultivating Coordinated efforts: Viable admittance to equity requires cooperation among lawful foundations, NGOs, people group associations, and different partners. Constructing and supporting organizations can enhance the effect of drives and make a more strong methodology.

Guaranteeing Social Awareness: Drives should be socially delicate and receptive to the interesting necessities of different networks. This includes thinking about semantic variety, social subtleties, and fluctuating degrees of lawful proficiency inside various populaces.

7.2 Legal aid programs, awareness campaigns, and community outreach efforts

Admittance to equity is a principal right that guarantees people can look for change, safeguard their privileges, and take part genuinely in legitimate cycles. Lawful guide programs, mindfulness missions, and local area outreach endeavors stand as vital support points in the undertaking to make equity open to all residents. These drives address monetary, educational, and fundamental hindrances, enabling people to explore the overall set of laws and attest their freedoms. This investigation dives into the meaning of legitimate guide programs, the effect of mindfulness crusades, and the groundbreaking job of local area outreach in cultivating a more comprehensive and fair equity framework.

1. **Legitimate Guide Projects:**

   Legitimate guide programs structure the foundation of endeavors to connect the equity hole, giving basic lawful help to people who can't bear the cost of private portrayal. These projects are intended to guarantee that monetary limitations don't hinder admittance to equity. Key components of legitimate guide programs include:

   Monetary Availability: Lawful guide programs focus on monetary openness by offering free or minimal expense legitimate administrations to people with restricted implies. This guarantees that financial boundaries don't block people from looking for lawful cures or partaking in legitimate cycles.

   Extent of Legitimate Guide: Legitimate guide isn't bound to explicit areas of regulation; rather, it envelops an expansive range, including common, criminal, and regulatory issues. This thorough methodology guarantees that people confronting assorted legitimate difficulties can profit themselves of help.

   Portrayal and Counsel: Legitimate guide programs frequently give direct portrayal by lawful experts in court procedures. Also, they offer legitimate counsel, conferences, and help with lawful documentation, engaging people to explore complex legitimate cycles.

   Local area Lawful Facilities: People group based legitimate centers, frequently associated with legitimate guide associations, bring lawful administrations straightforwardly to networks. These centers act as open center points where people can look for direction, go to studios, and get help customized to their particular lawful necessities.

   Cooperation with Free Endeavors: Legitimate guide programs frequently team up with free drives, utilizing the ability of volunteer attorneys to grow the compass of lawful help. This joint effort guarantees a more extensive pool of lawful experts adding to the conveyance of administrations.

   Designated Drives for Weak Gatherings: Legitimate guide programs perceive the one of a kind difficulties looked by powerless and minimized populaces. Drives might be custom-made to address the particular lawful requirements of gatherings like outsiders, abusive behavior at home survivors, and people with inabilities.

   The effect of legitimate guide programs is broad, as they act as a life saver for people exploring lawful intricacies without the monetary means to get private portrayal. Through these projects, admittance to equity turns into an unmistakable reality for a different scope of residents.

2. **Mindfulness Missions:**

While legitimate guide programs address monetary obstructions, mindfulness crusades assume a significant part in defeating enlightening snags that thwart admittance to equity. Numerous people might know nothing about their freedoms, the accessible lawful assets, or how to explore the overall set of laws. Mindfulness crusades act as an impetus for informed direction and dynamic cooperation in lawful cycles:

Publicizing Lawful Privileges: Mindfulness crusades center around publicizing legitimate freedoms and teaching residents about the lawful roads accessible to them. Through media channels, local area occasions, and online stages, these missions spread data that engages people to go with informed choices.

Advancing Legitimate Proficiency: Lawful education is a foundation of admittance to equity. Mindfulness crusades expect to upgrade legitimate proficiency by separating complex lawful ideas into effectively justifiable data. This remembers giving direction to normal lawful issues, making sense of court strategies, and offering assets for additional learning.

Tending to Marks of shame and Fantasies: Confusions and marks of disgrace encompassing the overall set of laws can discourage people from looking for help. Mindfulness crusades work to disperse fantasies, lessen shame, and establish a climate where people feel positive about moving toward lawful experts for help.

Using Different Media Stages: To contact a wide crowd, mindfulness crusades influence different media stages, including TV, radio, online entertainment, and print. Joint efforts with powerhouses, local area pioneers, and big names enhance the message and draw in networks on a grassroots level.

Custom fitted Informing for Explicit Crowds: Perceiving the variety of networks, mindfulness crusades frequently tailor informing to address the remarkable requirements of explicit crowds. Socially delicate correspondence guarantees that people from various foundations can associate with and comprehend the data introduced.

Cooperation with Instructive Foundations: Cooperative endeavors with instructive organizations, like schools and colleges, work with the combination of lawful training into educational plans. This proactive methodology ingrains legitimate mindfulness at an early age, cultivating a culture of lawful proficiency.

By bringing issues to light about legitimate freedoms, methods, and accessible assets, these missions engage people to proactively draw in with the general set of laws. Informed residents are bound to look for ideal help, go with informed choices, and add to the general adequacy of the equity framework.

3. **Local area Effort Endeavors:**

Local area effort is a dynamic and intelligent technique that brings lawful administrations straightforwardly to networks. Past scattering data, local area outreach endeavors effectively draw in with people, fabricate trust, and address fundamental boundaries. Key parts of local area outreach include:

Versatile Lawful Facilities: Portable legitimate centers are an unmistakable indication of local area outreach, taking lawful administrations making a course for reach underserved regions. These facilities give on-the-spot interviews, disperse enlightening materials, and interface people with legitimate guide assets.

Associations with Local area Associations: Coordinated efforts with neighborhood local area associations, charities, and grassroots developments upgrade the effect of effort endeavors. These organizations make an organization of help that reaches out past lawful guide to address more extensive local area needs.

Intuitive Studios and Classes: Studios and workshops directed in local area settings give intelligent stages to legitimate schooling. Subjects might go from understanding lawful privileges to viable direction on exploring explicit legitimate cycles.

Legitimate Strengthening Projects: People group outreach goes past quick lawful help to include more extensive lawful strengthening programs. These projects might include preparing local area individuals as paralegals, encouraging distributed encouraging groups of people, and building local area flexibility against lawful difficulties.

Socially Able Commitment: Social skill is necessary to compelling local area outreach. Drawing in with networks in a socially touchy way includes figuring out novel social settings, dialects, and customs. This approach assembles trust and guarantees that outreach endeavors are generally welcomed.

Resolving Foundational Issues: People group outreach endeavors frequently stretch out to resolving fundamental issues that add to legitimate difficulties. This might include upholding for strategy changes, teaming up with neighborhood specialists, and assembling local area individuals to address foundational shameful acts aggregately.

Local area effort is a proactive and grassroots methodology that perceives the interconnectedness of legitimate issues with more extensive local area elements. By cultivating trust, building connections, and effectively including networks in the equity cycle, outreach endeavors add to a more open and responsive general set of laws.

Difficulties and Contemplations:

While lawful guide programs, mindfulness missions, and local area outreach endeavors assume necessary parts in improving admittance to equity, certain difficulties and contemplations should be tended to:

Manageability of Effort Drives: Guaranteeing the maintainability of effort endeavors requires progressing responsibility and assets. Subsidizing, hierarchical help, and local area commitment are vital components for the drawn out effect of these drives.

Fitting Methodologies for Assorted People group: Networks are assorted, and exceed endeavors should be versatile to various social, phonetic, and financial settings. Fitting methodologies guarantees that effort is comprehensive and resounds with the exceptional requirements of every local area.

Assessment and Effect Estimation: Laying out components for assessing the effect of effort drives is fundamental. This includes following the quantity of people came to, surveying changes in lawful information, and understanding the more extensive local area influence over the long run.

Cooperation with Partners: Effective effort requires joint effort with different partners, including lawful establishments, government offices, NGOs, and local area pioneers. Building powerful organizations upgrades the compass and effect of effort endeavors.

Tending to Trust Deficiencies: In certain networks, verifiable doubt of legitimate organizations might represent a hindrance to compelling effort. Building trust requires straightforward correspondence, progressing commitment, and a pledge to resolving fundamental issues adding to doubt.

Utilizing Innovation for Effort: Incorporating innovation into outreach endeavors can upgrade reach and availability. Nonetheless, guaranteeing evenhanded admittance to innovation and tending to advanced proficiency variations are basic contemplations.

7.3 Assessment of the impact on marginalized communities

Surveying the Effect of Legitimate Guide Projects, Mindfulness Missions, and Local area Effort on Minimized People group: A Way to Strengthening

Admittance to equity is a principal right that ought to be general, yet verifiable differences have frequently left minimized networks confronting extra obstacles in exploring the overall set of laws. Legitimate guide programs, mindfulness missions, and local area outreach endeavors are necessary parts of more extensive drives pointed toward making equity more comprehensive and open. This evaluation dives into the effect of these drives on underestimated networks, analyzing the steps made in tending to variations, building trust, and engaging people inside these networks to declare their lawful privileges.

1. **Lawful Guide Projects and Underestimated People group:**

   Lawful guide programs act as a life saver for underestimated networks, which frequently face financial hindrances that obstruct their capacity to get private legitimate portrayal. The effect of lawful guide on minimized networks is complex:

   Defeating Monetary Hindrances: Minimized people group, including low-pay people and ethnic minorities, frequently face financial difficulties that hinder their admittance to legitimate portrayal. Lawful guide programs assume a significant part in defeating these boundaries by offering free or minimal expense legitimate administrations, guaranteeing that monetary requirements don't deny people their right to equity.

Tending to Foundational Treacheries: Minimized people group may excessively encounter fundamental shameful acts. Legitimate guide programs, by giving portrayal and support, add to testing and correcting these fundamental issues. This incorporates cases connected with lodging segregation, business privileges infringement, and inconsistent admittance to public administrations.

Engaging Weak Populaces: Legitimate guide drives tailor their administrations to address the extraordinary necessities of weak populaces inside underestimated networks, like overcomers of abusive behavior at home, foreigners, and people with incapacities. By offering specific help, lawful guide engages these people to explore complex legitimate cycles and look for review.

Diminishing Differences in Legitimate Portrayal: Variations in lawful portrayal add to inconsistent results inside the equity framework. Lawful guide programs endeavor to decrease these inconsistencies by guaranteeing that people from minimized networks approach capable legitimate experts who can successfully advocate for their sake.

Local area Lawful Facilities: People group based legitimate centers, frequently subsidiary with legitimate guide associations, bring legitimate administrations straightforwardly to minimized networks. These facilities act as open centers where people can look for direction, go to studios, and get help customized to their particular legitimate necessities, encouraging a feeling of local area commitment and backing.

While legitimate guide programs have taken critical steps, difficulties, for example, financing limits and the ability to fulfill the staggering need for administrations endure. Proceeded with promotion for expanded assets and foundational changes is fundamental to additionally reinforce the effect of legitimate guide on minimized networks.

2. **Mindfulness Missions and Underestimated People group:**

   Mindfulness crusades assume a significant part in destroying enlightening obstructions that may excessively influence underestimated networks. The effect of mindfulness crusades on these networks is apparent in a few key regions:

   Engaging Through Information: Mindfulness crusades engage people inside minimized networks by giving them information about their legitimate freedoms, accessible assets, and roads for looking for equity. Informed people are better prepared to explore the overall set of laws and go with informed choices.

Tending to Social Marks of shame: Underestimated people group might confront social marks of disgrace or misguided judgments that put commitment with the general set of laws down. Mindfulness crusades work to disperse these legends, lessen shame, and establish a climate where people feel sure about moving toward lawful experts for help.

Advancing Lawful Education: Legitimate proficiency is a basic part of admittance to equity. Mindfulness crusades center around advancing lawful education by improving on complex legitimate ideas, offering reasonable direction, and spreading data in dialects and arrangements open to different networks.

Fitting Informing to Assorted Crowds: Perceiving the variety inside minimized networks, mindfulness crusades tailor their informing to address the novel necessities of explicit crowds. Socially touchy correspondence guarantees that people from various foundations can associate with and comprehend the data introduced.

Coordinated efforts with Local area Pioneers: Joint efforts with local area pioneers and powerhouses upgrade the effect of mindfulness crusades inside minimized networks. Believed figures inside these networks can assume a significant part in scattering data, building trust, and empowering local area individuals to draw in with legitimate assets effectively.

Drawing in Youth and Instructive Foundations: Mindfulness crusades frequently expand their range by drawing in with youth and instructive establishments inside underestimated networks. This proactive methodology ingrains legitimate mindfulness at an early age, cultivating a culture of lawful proficiency and strengthening.

While mindfulness crusades contribute altogether to separating instructive obstructions, progressing endeavors are expected to guarantee supported commitment and address advancing difficulties, including the computerized partition and changing correspondence scenes.

3. **Local area Effort Endeavors and Minimized People group:**

Local area effort is a unique technique that effectively draws in with minimized networks, building trust, and tending to fundamental hindrances. The effect of local area outreach endeavors on these networks is clear in a few key aspects:

Building Trust: Trust is fundamental to successful local area outreach. By effectively captivating with networks, building connections, and showing a pledge to tending to their special necessities, outreach endeavors add to building trust between legitimate organizations and underestimated networks.

Portable Lawful Centers in Underserved Regions: Versatile legitimate facilities, a substantial sign of local area outreach, take legitimate administrations straightforwardly to underserved and underestimated regions. These facilities give on-the-spot conferences, disperse educational materials, and interface people with legitimate guide assets, guaranteeing that geographic hindrances don't frustrate admittance to equity.

Tending to Social Awareness: People group outreach endeavors are frequently planned considering social responsiveness. Grasping the exceptional social settings, dialects, and customs inside minimized networks is necessary to building successful effort techniques that resound with people's lived encounters.

Intelligent Studios and Courses: Studios and classes directed in local area settings give intuitive stages to legitimate schooling. These drives make spaces where people can effectively take part, seek clarification on pressing issues, and offer their interests, encouraging a feeling of pride and commitment inside the local area.

Legitimate Strengthening Projects: Past quick lawful help, local area outreach endeavors might incorporate more extensive legitimate strengthening programs. These projects include preparing local area individuals as paralegals, encouraging distributed encouraging groups of people, and building local area flexibility against lawful difficulties.

Promotion for Fundamental Changes: People group outreach endeavors frequently reach out to backing for foundational changes. By effectively captivating with neighborhood specialists, supporting for strategy changes, and preparing local area individuals, outreach drives add to tending to fundamental shameful acts that excessively influence underestimated networks.

While people group outreach endeavors have shown positive effects, continuous difficulties incorporate guaranteeing the maintainability of drives, tending to social subtleties, and adjusting systems to the advancing requirements of minimized networks.

Difficulties and Contemplations in Evaluating Effect on Underestimated People group:

Evaluating the effect of lawful guide programs, mindfulness missions, and local area outreach endeavors on minimized networks includes exploring a few difficulties and contemplations:

Variety Inside Minimized People group: Underestimated people group are not homogeneous, and drives should think about the variety inside these networks, including social, semantic, and financial contrasts. Fitting ways to deal with explicit necessities guarantees inclusivity.

Multifacetedness: People inside underestimated networks frequently experience converging types of segregation and disservice. Surveying influence requires a comprehension of these crossing factors, recognizing that specific gatherings might confront intensified difficulties.

Long haul Manageability: Guaranteeing the drawn out supportability of drives represents a test, especially with regards to financing limits and evolving needs. Methodologies for maintainability might include organizations, support for expanded assets, and a pledge to continuous assessment.

Computerized Gap: The computerized partition stays a huge thought, particularly in the time of innovation driven effort and mindfulness crusades. Guaranteeing impartial admittance to data and assets is vital to forestall further minimization of networks with restricted advanced admittance.

Social Capability: Accomplishing influence requires social ability in the plan and execution of drives. Grasping social subtleties, drawing in with local area pioneers, and adjusting systems to line up with social practices add to the viability of these drives.

Assessment Measurements: Creating strong measurements for assessing influence is fundamental. Measurements might remember changes for lawful proficiency, expanded commitment with legitimate assets, and substantial results like fruitful legitimate goals. Estimating influence requires a blend of quantitative and subjective evaluations.

Coordinated effort and Organizations: Compelling effect appraisal requires cooperation with partners, including legitimate foundations, government offices, NGOs, and local area pioneers. Building organizations improves the range and effect of drives, making a more durable and interconnected way to deal with equity.

Chapter 8

Accountability and Transparency

Responsibility and Straightforwardness in the Equity Framework: Mainstays of Trust and Authenticity

Responsibility and straightforwardness are basic rules that support the working of any equity framework. They are fundamental for encouraging public trust as well as for guaranteeing the authenticity of legitimate cycles and establishments. With regards to the law enforcement framework, responsibility and straightforwardness are central to maintaining law and order, safeguarding individual freedoms, and keeping up with the public's trust in the decency and honesty of judicial actions. This investigation digs into the basic jobs of responsibility and straightforwardness inside the equity framework, inspecting their importance, challenges, and the actions taken to improve them.

1. **Responsibility in the Equity Framework:**

   Responsibility inside the equity framework is a multi-layered idea that envelops different aspects, including the obligation of people, foundations, and the framework in general. Key parts of responsibility in the equity framework include:

   Legal Responsibility: Judges, as mediators of equity, are depended with the urgent errand of deciphering and applying the law. Legal responsibility includes guaranteeing that judges stay fair-minded, stick to moral guidelines, and are dependent upon systems that consider them responsible for their choices and lead. This responsibility isn't just fundamental for the believability of the legal executive yet additionally for protecting the privileges of people who precede the courts.

   Legal Responsibility: Examiners assume a focal part in the law enforcement process, addressing the state chasing equity. Legal responsibility involves considering examiners responsible for their activities, including the choice to charge, the introduction of proof, and cooperations with guard counsel. Guaranteeing reasonableness and honesty in the legal cycle is significant for maintaining the standards of equity.

Policing: Policing are entrusted with exploring violations, keeping public control, and maintaining the law. Responsibility in policing components to address unfortunate behavior, over the top utilization of power, and infringement of people's freedoms. Oversight bodies, inward issues units, and regular citizen audit sheets add to considering policing and keeping up with public certainty.

Institutional Responsibility: Past individual responsibility, there is a more extensive requirement for institutional responsibility inside the equity framework. This incorporates responsibility for fundamental issues, for example, case overabundance, shortcomings, and differences in the use of the law. Institutional responsibility guarantees that the equity framework overall is receptive to the necessities of society and ceaselessly looks for development.

Straightforwardness in Navigation: Straightforwardness in direction is a pivotal part of responsibility. It includes settling on legal choices, legal activities, and policing open and justifiable to the general population. Straightforward dynamic improves public comprehension as well as considers examination and guarantees that those answerable for regulating equity can be considered responsible for their activities.

Responsibility systems might incorporate legal audit, disciplinary cycles, and outside oversight bodies. The objective is to make a framework where those endowed with maintaining the law are liable for their activities, encouraging a culture of liability and supporting public trust.

2. **Straightforwardness in the Equity Framework:**

   Straightforwardness is a foundation of a fair and responsible equity framework. It includes transparency, clearness, and availability of data connected with legitimate cycles, choices, and institutional practices. Key components of straightforwardness in the equity framework include:

   Open Court Procedures: Open court procedures are a major part of straightforwardness in the equity framework. They permit people in general, media, and closely involved individuals to notice judicial procedures, guaranteeing that equity is controlled transparently and dependent upon public examination. Exemptions for open court standards are made in unambiguous conditions to safeguard delicate data or individual protection.

   Community to Lawful Data: Straightforwardness is upgraded when legitimate data is open to general society. This incorporates court records, lawful conclusions, and resolutions. Giving community to lawful data guarantees that people can grasp the legitimate structure, follow legitimate turns of events, and evaluate the reasonableness of legitimate cycles.

Media Access and Revealing: The media assume an essential part in guaranteeing straightforwardness by covering official procedures and choices. Media admittance to courts and authoritative records considers the dispersal of data to general society, adding to an educated populace. Capable reporting adds to public comprehension and investigation of the equity framework.

Exposure of Proof: Straightforwardness requires the divulgence of pertinent proof in judicial procedures. Investigators have an obligation to reveal proof to the safeguard, guaranteeing a fair preliminary. This guideline, known as the Brady rule, is fundamental for forestalling unfair convictions and maintaining the respectability of the law enforcement process.

Autonomous Oversight Bodies: Free oversight bodies, like ombudsman workplaces or inspectorates, add to straightforwardness by leading audits and examinations concerning charges of wrongdoing or fundamental issues inside the equity framework. These bodies act as outside components for considering organizations responsible and guaranteeing straightforwardness in their tasks.

Clear and Reasonable Lawful Cycles: Straightforwardness is additionally about making legitimate cycles understood and justifiable to people in general. Improving on legitimate language, giving data on lawful freedoms, and offering direction on exploring the equity framework add to a straightforward and open lawful climate.

Straightforwardness not just fills in as a shield against maltreatments of force yet in addition advances public trust in the equity framework. By permitting people to comprehend and examine lawful cycles, straightforwardness encourages a feeling of responsibility and supports the standards of equity and decency.

3. **Challenges in Accomplishing Responsibility and Straightforwardness:** While responsibility and straightforwardness are fundamental standards, accomplishing them inside the equity framework isn't without challenges. A portion of the key difficulties include:

Adjusting Security and Receptiveness: Adjusting the requirement for straightforwardness with protection contemplations is a continuous test. Certain legal procedures include delicate data, and keeping a harmony among transparency and it is pivotal to safeguard individual protection. Finding some kind of harmony requires cautious thought of the particular conditions and the standards in question.

Protection from Change: The equity framework, similar to any organization, may confront protection from change. Carrying out straightforwardness measures, responsibility components, and changes might experience opposition from inside the framework. Conquering opposition requires initiative, social movements, and a promise to consistent improvement.

Asset Requirements: Sufficient assets are important to carry out straightforwardness gauges successfully. This remembers speculations for innovation for community to lawful data, subsidizing for oversight bodies, and preparing for legitimate experts. Asset imperatives can thwart the full acknowledgment of straightforwardness objectives.

Complex Legitimate Cycles: Lawful cycles are intrinsically perplexing, and improving on them without compromising exactness can challenge. Making legitimate data more available to people in general expects endeavors to make an interpretation of perplexing lawful language into plain language, giving direction, and utilizing innovation to upgrade getting it.

Public Discernment and Trust: Public impression of the equity framework can affect the degree of confidence in its straightforwardness and responsibility. Negative discernments, whether established in real offense or falsehood, can disintegrate public trust. Constructing and keeping up with trust require proactive correspondence, responsiveness to worries, and a pledge to tending to genuine complaints.

Guaranteeing Consistency: Accomplishing consistency and consistency in straightforwardness rehearses across various wards and overall sets of laws is a test. Varieties in legitimate customs, rehearses, and mechanical framework can add to variations in the degree of straightforwardness. Blending rehearses and advancing best principles are continuous contemplations.

Tending to these difficulties requires an extensive and cooperative methodology including legitimate experts, policymakers, common society, and the general population. Beating opposition, designating assets decisively, and encouraging a culture of receptiveness are key stages toward accomplishing more noteworthy responsibility and straightforwardness inside the equity framework.

4. **Measures to Improve Responsibility and Straightforwardness:**

Endeavors to improve responsibility and straightforwardness inside the equity framework include a scope of measures and changes. A portion of the key drives include:

Innovation for Straightforwardness: Utilizing innovation is an extraordinary method for improving straightforwardness. Online stages for getting to court records, electronic documenting frameworks, and advanced specialized devices add to making lawful cycles more straightforward and open to people in general.

Preparing and Schooling: Giving preparation and instruction to legitimate experts, including judges, investigators, and policing, is significant for cultivating a culture of responsibility. Preparing projects can zero in on moral norms, the significance of straightforwardness, and the job of legitimate experts in maintaining the standards of equity.

Autonomous Oversight Bodies: Reinforcing free oversight bodies upgrades responsibility by giving outside systems to auditing protests, exploring offense, and guaranteeing adherence to moral norms. These bodies ought to have the position to suggest disciplinary activities and fundamental changes.

Local area Commitment: Effectively captivating with the local area adds to straightforwardness and fabricates public trust. Local area outreach programs, official Q&A events, and instructive drives permit legitimate experts to associate with the general population, address concerns, and make sense of lawful cycles in open terms.

Informant Assurance: Laying out powerful informant security components supports people inside the equity framework to offer facts about offense or exploitative practices. Informant assurance shields people who uncover bad behavior and adds to responsibility.

Normal Reviews and Evaluations: Directing customary reviews and evaluations of legitimate cycles and organizations gives an efficient method for distinguishing regions for development. These appraisals can be inward or completed by outer specialists, adding to progressing endeavors to improve responsibility and straightforwardness.

Clear Correspondence Procedures: Straightforward correspondence systems are fundamental for passing on data about lawful cycles, choices, and changes to general society. Clear and open correspondence demystifies the general set of laws, scatter misguided judgments, and encourage public comprehension.

Legitimate Guide and Admittance to Equity: Reinforcing lawful guide programs and guaranteeing admittance to equity for all people, including underestimated networks, is basic to responsibility. At the point when people approach lawful portrayal and assets, they are better prepared to challenge shameful acts and consider the framework responsible.

Regulative Changes: Official changes can assume a significant part in improving responsibility and straightforwardness. Refreshing regulations to reflect contemporary norms, explaining methods, and integrating instruments for oversight add to a legitimate system that lines up with standards of equity.

These actions, when carried out on the whole, add to an equity framework that is more responsible, straightforward, and receptive to the requirements of society. Persistent assessment, transformation, and a pledge to the standards of equity are fundamental for supporting these endeavors after some time.

8.1 Lok Sabha's initiatives to promote transparency in the criminal justice system

Straightforwardness is the bedrock of a hearty and responsible law enforcement framework, cultivating public trust, guaranteeing reasonableness, and building up the standards of a vote based system. With regards to India, the Lok Sabha, as the lower place of Parliament, assumes a vital part in molding regulative changes and drives pointed toward upgrading straightforwardness inside the law enforcement framework. This investigation dives into Lok Sabha's earth shattering drives intended to advance straightforwardness, examine institutional practices, and reinforce the groundworks of the law enforcement framework in the country.

1. **Regulative Changes for Upgraded Straightforwardness:**

   Lok Sabha, as the regulative body liable for instituting regulations, has been at the very front of acquainting huge authoritative changes with improve straightforwardness inside the law enforcement framework. Key drives include:

   Right to Data Act (RTI): The Right to Data Act, ordered by the Parliament in 2005, is a milestone piece of regulation that enables residents to look for data from public specialists, including those inside the law enforcement framework. This act has been instrumental in opening up beforehand murky institutional practices to public examination, empowering residents to get to imperative data connected with legal procedures, choices, and authoritative cycles.

   Alterations to Criminal Strategy Code (CrPC): Lok Sabha has attempted changes to the Criminal System Code to smooth out and modernize legitimate cycles. These changes frequently integrate arrangements pointed toward improving straightforwardness, like the divulgence of proof, open court procedures, and systems for giving data to general society. These changes add to making legitimate cycles more open and justifiable to people in general.

   Witness Security Regulations: Perceiving the significance of witness assurance in guaranteeing fair preliminaries and reinforcing straightforwardness, Lok Sabha has been effectively engaged with the definition of witness insurance regulations. These regulations mean to establish a safe climate for observers to approach unafraid of terrorizing, consequently adding to the general straightforwardness of judicial procedures.

   Presentation of Innovation in Legitimate Cycles: Lok Sabha has supported the reconciliation of innovation in lawful cycles to improve proficiency and straightforwardness. Drives, for example, the digitization of court records, electronic documenting frameworks, and online admittance to case data add to making legal actions more straightforward and open to the general population.

2. **Parliamentary Oversight and Responsibility:**

   Lok Sabha, as the administrative arm of the public authority, practices oversight over the presidential branch, including organizations inside the law enforcement framework. Key drives advancing oversight and responsibility include:

Parliamentary Boards of trustees: Lok Sabha is different parliamentary councils, for example, the Standing Panel on Home Undertakings and the Council on Staff, Public Complaints, Regulation and Equity, which assume an essential part in examining the working of organizations inside the law enforcement framework. These boards direct requests, look for reports, and make proposals to guarantee responsibility and straightforwardness.

Question Hour and Discussions: Lok Sabha gives a stage to individuals to bring questions and connect up in discusses connected with the law enforcement framework. This parliamentary talk fills in as a component for considering the public authority responsible, looking for explanations, and evoking data that adds to public comprehension of legitimate cycles.

Reports and Proposals: Parliamentary panels, through their considerations, produce reports and suggestions resolving issues inside the law enforcement framework. These reports act as important assets for recognizing areas of progress, proposing changes, and advancing straightforwardness in institutional practices.

3. **Computerized Drives and Public Commitment:**

Lok Sabha has embraced computerized drives to draw in with people in general, scatter data, and advance straightforwardness inside the law enforcement framework. Key computerized drives include:

Online Entrances for Legitimate Data: Lok Sabha has upheld the improvement of online entryways that give admittance to lawful data, including resolutions, court choices, and procedural rules. These entryways act as important assets for the general population, legitimate experts, and specialists, adding to straightforwardness in lawful cycles.

Live Gushing of Parliamentary Procedures: To improve straightforwardness and public commitment, Lok Sabha has presented the live spilling of parliamentary procedures. This drive permits residents to notice discussions, conversations, and dynamic cycles connected with lawful changes and law enforcement drives.

Public Discussions and Criticism: Lok Sabha has started public meetings and looked for input on proposed authoritative changes connected with the law enforcement framework. This comprehensive methodology permits residents to contribute their points of view, voice concerns, and partake in the molding of legitimate systems, subsequently encouraging straightforwardness and popularity based commitment.

4. **Guaranteeing Legal Responsibility:**

Advancing straightforwardness inside the law enforcement framework requires resolving issues connected with legal responsibility. Lok Sabha has been effectively associated with drives pointed toward guaranteeing responsibility inside the legal executive, including:

Legal Arrangements and Responsibility Bill: Lok Sabha has thought on and acquainted bills related with legal arrangements and responsibility. These bills look to lay out components for straightforward and responsible cycles in the choice and direct of judges, building up the standards of a free and fair legal executive.

Cooperation in Worldwide Shows: Lok Sabha's commitment to worldwide shows, like the Unified Countries Show against Defilement (UNCAC), highlights its obligation to worldwide norms of straightforwardness and responsibility. Cooperation in these shows considers the trading of best practices and the joining of worldwide standards into homegrown lawful structures.

5. **Tending to Overabundance of Cases:**

   Lok Sabha perceives the meaning of tending to the overabundance of cases as a urgent component of improving straightforwardness and proficiency inside the law enforcement framework. Drives to address case overabundance include:

   Quick Track Courts: Lok Sabha has upheld the foundation of quick track courts to speed up the settlement of specific classes of cases. These courts are intended to address the overabundance of cases, particularly those connected with grievous violations, and add to guaranteeing convenient and straightforward equity.

   Designation of Assets: Lok Sabha distributes assets and assets to upgrade the foundation and limit of the legal executive. Interests in the foundation of extra courts, arrangement of additional adjudicators, and sending of mechanical arrangements add to tending to the overabundance and working on the productivity of legitimate cycles.

6. **Public Mindfulness and Legitimate Education Projects:**

Advancing straightforwardness requires an educated and drew in populace. Lok Sabha has been instrumental in supporting drives zeroed in on open mindfulness and legitimate education, including:

Legitimate Guide Projects: Lok Sabha upholds and advances lawful guide programs pointed toward giving help to people who might not have the monetary means to get to legitimate portrayal. Lawful guide programs add to guaranteeing that all people approach equity, cultivating straightforwardness and decency.

Public Mindfulness Missions: Lok Sabha starts and supports public mindfulness missions to illuminate residents about their legitimate privileges, accessible assets, and the working of the law enforcement framework. These missions add to demystifying legitimate cycles, advancing straightforwardness, and empowering public commitment.

Fuse of Legitimate Training in School Educational plans: Perceiving the significance of early lawful schooling, Lok Sabha advocates for the consolidation of lawful proficiency programs into school educational programs. By acquainting understudies with essential legitimate ideas and cycles, this drive expects to construct a groundwork of lawful mindfulness since early on.

Difficulties and Contemplations:

While Lok Sabha's drives are exemplary, a few difficulties and contemplations should be addressed to guarantee the supported outcome of straightforwardness advancing measures:

Asset Imperatives: Sufficient allotment of assets is vital for the successful execution of straightforwardness drives. Asset requirements can ruin the sending of innovation, foundation of quick track courts, and the general improvement of framework inside the law enforcement framework.

Protection from Changes: Protection from changes, both inside the framework and in open discernment, represents a test. Institutional obstruction, feeling of dread toward change, and doubt from different partners might block the reception of straightforwardness upgrading measures.

Intricacy of Lawful Cycles: The intrinsic intricacy of legitimate cycles presents a test in making them more straightforward and open to the general population. Endeavors to improve on legitimate language, smooth out systems, and upgrade understanding should explore the complicated idea of lawful structures.

Guaranteeing Fair Access: Guaranteeing that straightforwardness estimates benefit all areas of society, including minimized networks, is basic. Endeavors should be made to connect the computerized partition, give legitimate data in numerous dialects, and address financial obstructions to getting to lawful assets.

Adjusting Protection and Receptiveness: Accomplishing the right harmony between security contemplations and the transparency expected for straightforwardness is a sensitive undertaking. Measures that uncover delicate data might have potentially negative results, requiring cautious consideration of privacy safeguards

8.2 Introduction of accountability mechanisms for law enforcement agencies

The adequacy of any equity framework relies on the responsibility of its policing. Policing assume a urgent part in keeping public control, forestalling and researching wrongdoings, and maintaining law and order. Responsibility instruments inside these offices are fundamental to guarantee that their activities line up with legitimate guidelines, regard individual privileges, and keep up with the public's trust. This investigation dives into the basic of presenting responsibility instruments for policing, looking at their importance, challenges, and the groundbreaking effect they can have on the equity framework.

1. **The Meaning of Responsibility in Policing:**

   Responsibility is the key part that maintains the respectability and validity of policing. A few key viewpoints highlight the meaning of responsibility in this unique circumstance:

   Public Trust and Certainty: Policing get their authenticity from the trust and certainty of the public they serve. Responsibility components are instrumental in encouraging and keeping up with this trust by guaranteeing that policing are straightforward, fair, and dependent upon examination.

   Security of Individual Freedoms: Responsibility fills in as a shield against likely maltreatments of force and infringement of individual privileges. By considering policing, social orders shield residents from outlandish interruptions, manhandles, and erratic activities, in this manner maintaining the standards of equity and law and order.

   Discouragement of Wrongdoing: Clear responsibility systems go about as a hindrance against unfortunate behavior inside policing. Realizing that activities are dependent upon examination and results urges adherence to moral guidelines and legitimate practices.

   Improved Adequacy: Responsibility isn't contradictory to powerful policing, it supplements it. Offices that are responsible are better situated to collect open participation, knowledge, and backing, at last improving their viability in forestalling and tackling wrongdoings.

   Fair and Evenhanded Equity: Responsibility adds to the organization of fair and impartial equity. At the point when policing are considered responsible, people are bound to get fair-minded treatment, no matter what their experience, guaranteeing an equity framework that is oblivious to inclination and segregation.

2. **Challenges in Carrying out Responsibility Systems:**

   While the significance of responsibility is undisputed, the execution of viable systems experiences different difficulties:

   Inner Opposition: Protection from responsibility measures might arise inside policing. Social standards, protection from change, and worries about subverting assurance can impede the acknowledgment of responsibility systems.

   Absence of Assets: Satisfactory assets, both concerning subsidizing and innovation, are important for the execution of responsibility components. The absence of assets can block the advancement of straightforward frameworks, preparing projects, and oversight bodies.

   Political Obstruction: Political impedance in policing represents a test to responsibility. At times, policing may confront strain to act in a way lined up with political plans as opposed to sticking stringently to lawful and moral guidelines.

Intricacy of Cases: Exploring and tending to wrongdoing inside policing be complicated, especially when cases include delicate data or perplexing lawful contemplations. Adjusting the requirement for straightforwardness with the assurance of specific subtleties can challenge.

Adjusting Freedom and Oversight: Finding some kind of harmony between keeping up with the freedom of policing and giving outside oversight is a fragile undertaking. Responsibility systems should be powerful without compromising the independence required for viable policing.

3. **Presentation of Responsibility Components:**

Endeavors to present responsibility components for policing include a complex methodology pointed toward tending to difficulties and advancing straightforwardness. Key drives include:

Free Oversight Bodies: The foundation of autonomous oversight bodies is a crucial stage in presenting responsibility systems. These bodies, frequently regular citizen survey sheets or ombudsman workplaces, act as outside elements entrusted with examining objections, evaluating activities, and guaranteeing adherence to legitimate and moral norms.

Body-Worn Cameras: The broad reception of body-worn cameras by cops is an innovative drive that upgrades responsibility. These cameras record communications among officials and general society, giving a goal record that can be audited if there should arise an occurrence of debates or charges of wrongdoing.

Informant Assurance: Making hearty informant insurance components supports people inside policing offer facts about unfortunate behavior unafraid of counter. Informant insurance defends the individuals who uncover bad behavior, encouraging a culture of responsibility.

Local area Policing and Commitment: Encouraging people group policing drives upgrades responsibility by laying out sure connections between policing and the networks they serve. Drawing in with the local area fabricates trust, empowers participation, and gives a channel to public contribution on policing rehearses.

Inner Undertakings Units: Reinforcing interior issues units inside policing is fundamental for tending to unfortunate behavior from the inside. These units examine claims of bad behavior, keep up with interior discipline, and add to a culture of responsibility.

Preparing Projects: Executing exhaustive preparation programs is pivotal for ingraining a culture of responsibility inside policing. Preparing ought to envelop lawful principles, moral contemplations, de-heightening strategies, and social awareness, guaranteeing that officials are completely ready to explore complex circumstances.

4. **Utilization of Innovation in Responsibility:**

Mechanical headways offer groundbreaking open doors for improving responsibility inside policing:

Advanced Proof Administration: Carrying out computerized proof administration frameworks guarantees the safe stockpiling and recovery of advanced proof, including body camera film, observation accounts, and scientific information. This innovation works with straightforwardness and gives a coordinated stage to responsibility.

Information Examination for Oversight: Utilizing information investigation permits oversight bodies to break down examples, patterns, and occurrences inside policing. Information driven oversight can recognize areas of concern, screen execution, and add to confirm based direction.

Online Grievance Entrances: Laying out web-based gateways for recording objections against policing advances straightforwardness and availability. Residents can submit objections and give criticism, adding to a more comprehensive and responsible way to deal with policing.

Prescient Policing Innovation: While dubious, prescient policing innovation can be outfit to upgrade responsibility by straightforwardly showing how calculations are utilized and guaranteeing that they don't sustain predispositions or unfair practices.

5. **Global Norms and Best Practices:**

Drawing on worldwide guidelines and best practices is fundamental to forming successful responsibility instruments:

Adherence to Basic liberties Standards: Adjusting responsibility systems to worldwide common freedoms standards guarantees that policing regard the respect and privileges of people. This incorporates keeping away from inconsistent confinement, forestalling torment, and shielding the right to a fair preliminary.

Joining of Worldwide Oversight Models: Considering and consolidating fruitful worldwide oversight models gives significant experiences. Gaining from the encounters of different nations can assist with fitting responsibility instruments to line up with the particular requirements and difficulties of a specific ward.

Cooperation in Peaceful accords: Partaking in peaceful accords and shows on policing, like the Unified Countries Show Against Torment, highlights a guarantee to worldwide norms and works with coordinated effort in resolving transnational issues.

6. **Local area Criticism and Effect Evaluation:**

Effectively looking for local area criticism and leading effect appraisals are vital parts of responsibility:

Local area Survey Sheets: Laying out local area audit sheets or warning boards permits residents to take part in the oversight of policing. These sheets give significant points of view, guarantee local area portrayal, and add to responsibility.

Ordinary Effect Appraisals: Directing customary effect evaluations of responsibility components recognizes their viability and regions for development. Evaluations ought to incorporate criticism from the local area, information on official direct, and the results of examinations.

8.3 Demonstrating increased trust in the justice system

Trust in the equity framework is vital for the working of any fair society. At the point when residents accept that the general set of laws is fair, unbiased, and open, it cultivates a feeling of safety, supports collaboration, and maintains law and order. In any case, fabricating and keeping up with trust in the equity framework is a complicated test that requires proactive measures, straightforwardness, and local area commitment. This investigation dives into methodologies pointed toward exhibiting expanded trust in the equity framework, looking at the complex methodologies that can add to improved public certainty.

Straightforwardness and Transparency:

Straightforwardness is a fundamental component for building trust in the equity framework. Transparency about legitimate cycles, independent direction, and institutional practices adds to the view of reasonableness and responsibility. Key parts of straightforwardness include:

Open Court Procedures: Directing court procedures in an open and available way permits the general population to observe equity in real life. Exemptions might be made for delicate data, however the default ought to be straightforwardness to impart public certainty.

Open Legitimate Data: Making lawful data, including rules, court choices, and procedural rules, effectively available to the public cultivates understanding and demystifies the lawful interaction. Online gateways and public libraries can act as significant assets.

Divulgence of Proof: Guaranteeing the revelation of applicable proof during legal procedures is fundamental. This standard maintains decency in preliminaries as well as builds up the possibility that equity is sought after with respectability.

Public Writing about Institutional Practices: Policing, courts, and remedial offices ought to routinely distribute gives an account of their practices, results, and any restorative means taken. This straightforward announcing constructs responsibility and addresses worries inside the local area.

Local area Commitment and Cooperation:

Connecting with the local area in the equity framework advances a feeling of pride, understanding, and coordinated effort. Drives that empower local area cooperation include:

Local area Policing: Laying major areas of strength for out between policing and the networks they serve through local area policing drives cultivates common trust. Officials effectively captivating with occupants, going to local gatherings, and addressing concerns add to positive collaborations.

Resident Warning Sheets: Making resident warning sheets permits local area individuals to have a voice in policing strategies and practices. These sheets give a stage to open discourse, permitting residents to communicate concerns and team up with policing arrangements.

Public Discussions and Municipal centers: Facilitating public gatherings, official Q&A events, and interactive discussions with legitimate experts and policing give chances to coordinate correspondence. This open discourse helps address local area concerns, explain legitimate cycles, and construct getting it.

Instructive Projects: Carrying out instructive projects that attention on lawful education, privileges, and the operations of the equity framework can engage residents. Studios, courses, and effort programs add to a more educated and connected with local area.

Responsibility Instruments:

Exhibiting a guarantee to responsibility inside the equity framework is critical for building trust. Responsibility systems include:

Free Oversight Bodies: Laying out autonomous oversight bodies, for example, non military personnel audit sheets or ombudsman workplaces, gives outside examination of policing. These bodies examine grievances, survey rehearses, and add to responsibility.

Informant Security: Making powerful informant insurance instruments energizes people inside the equity framework to offer data about unfortunate behavior or inconsistencies. This security guarantees that the individuals who uncover bad behavior are protected from counter.

Interior Undertakings Units: Reinforcing inward undertakings units inside policing guarantees that wrongdoing is tended to from the inside. These units explore claims, keep up with inside discipline, and add to a culture of responsibility.

Execution Assessment and Reviews: Routinely assessing the presentation of legitimate experts, policing, and remedial offices through reviews guarantees adherence to moral and lawful principles. Publicizing the results of these assessments upgrades straightforwardness.

Mechanical Advancements:

Embracing innovative progressions can improve straightforwardness, productivity, and responsibility inside the equity framework. Innovative arrangements include:

Computerized Proof Administration: Executing frameworks for the safe stockpiling and recovery of advanced proof, including body-worn camera film and measurable information, guarantees straightforwardness and responsibility in examinations.

Online Entries for Lawful Data: Creating easy to use online entryways that give legitimate data, court timetables, and case refreshes empowers general society to effortlessly get to applicable data.

Body-Worn Cameras: The far reaching utilization of body-worn cameras by policemen gives a goal record of connections. This innovation upgrades responsibility and fills in as a significant device for surveying episodes.

Information Investigation for Oversight: Utilizing information examination permits oversight bodies to break down examples, patterns, and episodes inside the equity framework. This information driven approach can recognize regions for development and screen the effect of strategy changes.

Social Ability and Variety:

Perceiving and regarding the social variety inside networks is fundamental for building trust. Systems include:

Social Responsiveness Preparing: Giving social awareness preparing to legitimate experts and policemen improves how they might interpret assorted networks. This preparing adds to fair and evenhanded treatment.

Various Portrayal: Guaranteeing variety in the enrollment and advancement of legitimate experts, policemen, and legal executive individuals mirrors the networks they serve. Various portrayal encourages trust and certainty among various segment gatherings.

Language Access: Giving language access administrations, including translators and deciphered materials, guarantees that people with restricted English capability can completely take part in legitimate cycles. This comprehensive methodology improves availability and trust.

Helpful Equity Projects:

Presenting helpful equity projects can reshape the equity framework's methodology by zeroing in on fixing hurt, recuperating connections, and including the local area. Parts of supportive equity include:

Local area Based Arrangements: Including the local area in making answers for wrongdoers underscores the aggregate liability regarding keeping an equitable and safe society.

Casualty Wrongdoer Exchanges: Working with discoursed among casualties and guilty parties takes into account grasping, compassion, and the chance for compensation. This cycle adds to recuperating and compromise.

Preventive Measures: Underlining preventive measures and recovery over correctional methodologies lines up with supportive equity standards. Programs that address the underlying drivers of wrongdoing add to long haul local area prosperity.

Chapter 9

Conclusion

In exploring the multifaceted scene of law enforcement, the excursion towards modernization and change is a demonstration of the aggregate responsibility of partners, especially the Lok Sabha, in molding an equity framework that is straightforward, responsible, and receptive to the requirements of society. The multilayered investigation of drives, challenges, and groundbreaking estimates highlights the intricacy of the main job and the meaning of cultivating public trust. As we close this complete assessment, a few key topics arise, mirroring the way ahead for a dependable and comprehensive equity framework.

A Change in outlook towards Modernization:

The modernization of the law enforcement framework, led by the Lok Sabha, addresses a change in outlook that rises above conventional methodologies. Embracing innovation, regulative changes, and creative practices, the Lok Sabha has situated itself as an impetus for change. The obligation to straightforwardness, proficiency, and decency has laid the preparation for a framework that adjusts to contemporary difficulties and expects the developing requirements of society.

Recognizing and Tending to Difficulties:

A basic part of the modernization venture is the affirmation and proactive tending to of difficulties inside the law enforcement framework. From case build-up and obsolete innovation to foundational shortcomings, the Lok Sabha has shown a sharp familiarity with the obstacles obstructing the framework's viability. By facing these difficulties head-on, drives have been created to upgrade framework, smooth out methods, and brace the framework's establishment.

The Job of Lok Sabha in Starting Changes:

Vital to the groundbreaking story is the essential pretended by the Lok Sabha in starting and supporting changes. The regulative body's obligation to regulative changes, oversight, and the presentation of forward-looking strategies has established the vibe for an equity framework that isn't just established in lawfulness but at the same time is lined up with the standards of equity, decency, and common liberties. The Lok Sabha's vision for change fills in as a directing power in molding the direction of the law enforcement framework.

Building Trust through Responsibility and Straightforwardness:

Trust is the foundation whereupon a vigorous and strong equity framework is constructed. The drives zeroed in on responsibility and straightforwardness, going from free oversight bodies to mechanical combinations, exhibit a promise to receptiveness and decency. These systems are not simply procedural; they represent a significant comprehension that public trust is procured through self evident adherence to moral norms, fair independent direction, and a certified obligation to the prosperity of the local area.

Local area Commitment as an Impetus for Change:

The commitment of networks inside the equity framework is a strong impetus for change. Local area policing, resident warning sheets, and public discussions add to a participatory model where the worries, assumptions, and bits of knowledge of residents are incorporated into the dynamic cycles. This comprehensive methodology cultivates a feeling of pride as well as guarantees that the equity framework is receptive to the different requirements of the populace it serves.

Utilizing Innovation for Productivity and Openness:

The coordination of innovation arises as a critical subject in the journey for a modernized equity framework. From computerized proof administration to online entryways for legitimate data, innovation is utilized not as a simple device but rather as an extraordinary power that improves productivity, openness, and responsibility. The cautious harmony between mechanical headways and human-driven approaches guarantees that advancements contribute decidedly to the general equity experience.

Supportive Equity as a Human-Driven Approach:

The accentuation on supportive equity programs mirrors a takeoff from reformatory models towards a human-driven approach. By zeroing in on fixing hurt, mending connections, and including networks in the goal cycle, supportive equity lines up with the standards of sympathy, recovery, and counteraction. This comprehensive methodology perceives the interconnectedness of people inside society and underlines long haul arrangements over corrective measures.

Social Capability and Variety as Goals:

Recognizing and regarding the social variety inside networks isn't simply a moral basic yet an essential need for building trust. Social responsiveness preparing, different portrayal, and language access drives show a pledge to impartial treatment and a comprehension that equity should be open and interesting to people from varying backgrounds.

The Continuous Advancement of the Equity Framework:

The modernization and change of the law enforcement framework are not static endpoints but rather a continuous development. Ceaseless assessment, transformation, and a responsiveness to arising difficulties are fundamental for supporting the energy towards a framework that stands as a reference point of equity. The obligation to remaining sensitive to cultural requirements, embracing criticism, and consolidating illustrations gained from the two triumphs and mishaps are necessary to this unique interaction.

The Cooperative Idea of Change:

At long last, the account of law enforcement modernization and change highlights the cooperative idea of the undertaking. It is a combination of endeavors from regulative bodies, policing, legitimate experts, local area individuals, and mechanical trend-setters. The aggregate obligation to a common vision — an equity framework that rouses certainty, exemplifies reasonableness, and serves the interests of all — is a demonstration of the force of coordinated effort in affecting positive cultural change.

9.1 Recap of Lok Sabha's initiatives and their impact on modernizing criminal justice

As we dig into a reiteration of the Lok Sabha's drives pointed toward modernizing the law enforcement framework in India, a convincing story arises — one of efficient change, visionary strategy making, and an immovable obligation to building an equity framework that is responsive, straightforward, and impartial. The Lok Sabha, as the essential regulative body in India, plays had a crucial impact in guiding the course of progress, tending to difficulties, and imagining a future where the law enforcement framework adjusts consistently with the developing requirements of society.

Administrative Changes:

At the core of the Lok Sabha's modernization plan lies a progression of regulative changes intended to recalibrate the lawful scene. These changes are not simple corrections; they address a significant change in legitimate standards, adjusting the law to contemporary qualities and worldwide prescribed procedures. Whether it be changes in criminal regulations, strategies, or punishments, the Lok Sabha's administrative drives signal a pledge to encouraging a legitimate system that isn't just vigorous yet in addition intelligent of the standards of equity and decency.

Influence Investigation of Authoritative Changes:

A basic part of the Lok Sabha's modernization drives is the thorough effect investigation of regulative changes. Understanding this present reality outcomes of legitimate changes is basic for informed direction. The Lok Sabha's obligation to confirm based policymaking guarantees that regulative changes are not executed in confinement but rather are important for an all encompassing technique to upgrade the proficiency and decency of the law enforcement framework.

Innovative Headways:

Embracing innovation as an impetus for change, the Lok Sabha has supported the joining of state of the art devices inside the law enforcement contraption. From computerized proof administration frameworks to the utilization of man-made brainpower and information examination, these mechanical headways are not seen as extravagances but rather as fundamental parts for further developing examination, upgrading straightforwardness, and guaranteeing that the equity framework works at the very front of advancement.

Computerized Stages and Man-made consciousness:

The Lok Sabha's push for computerized stages and man-made consciousness is extraordinary in its degree. These drives are not bound to a shallow modernization of cycles yet address a change in perspective in how data is made due, dissected, and used inside the equity framework. The imbuement of man-made brainpower into dynamic cycles mirrors a ground breaking approach, where information driven bits of knowledge add to more educated, effective, and fair results.

Challenges Tended to:

The Lok Sabha's drives are not oblivious in regards to the difficulties intrinsic in modernizing the law enforcement framework. By recognizing and tending to difficulties, for example, case overabundance, obsolete innovation, and insufficient foundation, the regulative body has shown a nuanced comprehension of the fundamental issues that thwart the framework's productivity. Every drive is a designated reaction to explicit difficulties, stressing a comprehensive way to deal with change.

Endeavors to Work on Legal Productivity:

Perceiving that the overabundance of cases is an inescapable issue, the Lok Sabha has carried out measures pointed toward working on legal proficiency. From the presentation of elective question goal systems to designated mediations to address case pendency, these endeavors mirror a pledge to quick and fair equity conveyance. The Lok Sabha's drives are not restricted to official changes but rather reach out to procedural upgrades that smooth out the adjudicative cycle.

Reinforcing Policing:

The Lok Sabha's emphasis on fortifying policing is an essential move towards building a more responsive and skilled power. Drives incorporate preparation programs, gear redesigns, and enrollment changes — each adding to a policing that isn't simply exceptional but at the same time is receptive to the developing idea of wrongdoing and public security challenges.

Mechanical Coordination in Policing:

The Lok Sabha's hug of mechanical coordination in policing is a foundation of modernization. The utilization of computerized stages, man-made brainpower, and information examination improves the analytical abilities of policing. This progress isn't just about staying aware of mechanical patterns yet about utilizing development to remain in front of arising difficulties in wrongdoing recognition, avoidance, and reaction.

Improving Admittance to Equity:

Perceiving that admittance to equity is certainly not a simple lawful standard however a crucial right, the Lok Sabha has presented drives pointed toward making the equity framework more open to all residents. From lawful guide projects to mindfulness missions and local area outreach endeavors, these drives encapsulate a pledge to democratizing admittance to legitimate assets and guaranteeing that equity isn't an honor yet a right accessible to each person.

Local area Commitment and Public Mindfulness:

The Lok Sabha's drives go past the regulative domain to draw in networks and raise public mindfulness effectively. Perceiving that an educated populace is an enabled populace, the Lok Sabha's endeavors incorporate local area policing, resident warning sheets, and public gatherings. These stages work with a discourse between the equity framework and people in general, encouraging a feeling of cooperation and shared liability.

Advancement of Responsibility and Straightforwardness:

Responsibility and straightforwardness are not simple trendy expressions but rather core values supporting the Lok Sabha's modernization plan. Drives, for example, free oversight bodies, informant insurance instruments, and execution assessments add to an equity framework that isn't simply responsible to the general population however effectively tries to keep up with the most elevated moral and legitimate principles.

Worldwide Principles and Best Practices:

Drawing motivation from worldwide norms and best practices, the Lok Sabha's drives are not separate however educated by a more extensive comprehension regarding equity frameworks around the world. Taking part in peaceful accords, consolidating oversight models from effective purviews, and sticking to basic liberties standards signal a guarantee to adjusting India's equity framework to the best the world brings to the table.

Supportive Equity and Human-Driven Approaches:

A particular component of the Lok Sabha's modernization drives is the accentuation on supportive equity and human-driven approaches. The acknowledgment that equity isn't just about discipline yet about mending, compromise, and forestalling recidivism is implanted in programs that include networks, work with casualty wrongdoer exchanges, and focus on preventive measures.

Building Confidence in the Equity Framework:

Maybe the most significant effect of the Lok Sabha's drives is the precise work to construct trust in the equity framework. All along, the accentuation on straightforwardness, local area commitment, and responsibility isn't just about legitimate cycles; it is tied in with developing a relationship of trust between the equity framework and the residents it serves.

9.2 Future prospects and ongoing challenges

As we consider what's in store possibilities and continuous moves in the excursion to modernize the law enforcement framework, it becomes obvious that while critical steps have been made, the way ahead is set apart by both commitment and intricacy. The Lok Sabha's drives, however extraordinary, are important for a continuous story, and as we peer into the future, a few key regions request thoughtfulness regarding guarantee the supported development of an equity framework that is evenhanded, effective, and receptive to the requirements of a powerful society.

Mechanical Development and Moral Contemplations:

The eventual fate of law enforcement is naturally connected to innovative development. The joining of man-made brainpower, information examination, and advanced stages will probably assume a considerably more urgent part in examinations, proof administration, and navigation. In any case, as innovation propels, moral contemplations become progressively basic. Finding some kind of harmony between utilizing the advantages of innovation and defending individual privileges, protection, and forestalling algorithmic inclination will be a constant test.

Guaranteeing Admittance to Equity for Underestimated People group:

While steps have been made in improving admittance to equity, guaranteeing that underestimated networks have impartial access stays a continuous test. The Lok Sabha's drives to advance mindfulness and effort are critical, yet supported endeavors are expected to address fundamental boundaries, financial variations, and social factors that might impede admittance to lawful assets for specific fragments of the populace.

Adjusting to Arising Wrongdoing Patterns:

Modernizing the law enforcement framework requires a proactive reaction to arising wrongdoing patterns. Cybercrime, transnational coordinated wrongdoing, and new types of criminal way of behaving require an equity framework that is dexterous and prepared to address novel difficulties. Regulation, analytical strategies, and global coordinated effort will assume significant parts in adjusting to and moderating the effect of advancing wrongdoing designs.

Information Security and Protection Concerns:

The rising dependence on computerized stages and information investigation delivers a bunch of difficulties connected with information security and protection. As the law enforcement framework embraces innovation, shielding touchy data, forestalling unapproved access, and laying out strong network protection measures become principal. Regulation and strategies should develop to make a legitimate system that guarantees the mindful and secure utilization of information.

Cultivating People group Driven Arrangements:

The fate of law enforcement lies in encouraging local area driven arrangements. Drives, for example, local area policing, resident warning sheets, and helpful equity projects ought to be additionally extended and refined. Engaging people group to effectively partake in forming the equity framework fabricates trust as well as adds to a more nuanced comprehension of nearby necessities and concerns.

Proceeded with Authoritative Changes:

Authoritative changes should stay a continuous interaction, receptive to cultural changes and developing lawful guidelines. The Lok Sabha's obligation to authoritative changes is praiseworthy, and the attention ought to persevere on refining regulations, shutting lawful provisos, and adjusting the legitimate system to line up with global accepted procedures while keeping up with social awareness.

Tending to Build-up and Court Effectiveness:

Notwithstanding endeavors to work on legal productivity, the excess of cases stays a tenacious test. What's in store requires a thorough system that consolidates procedural changes, mechanical arrangements, and asset distribution to resolve this issue. Embracing elective question goal components and investigating creative court the executives strategies will be significant in accomplishing a more productive equity conveyance framework.

Manageability of Mechanical Drives:

The effective mix of innovation is dependent upon its supportability. As innovation develops quickly, guaranteeing that advanced stages, computerized reasoning frameworks, and information investigation instruments remain refreshed, secure, and lined up with legitimate principles turns into a continuous goal. Interests in innovation ought to be joined by a strong system for support, refreshes, and consistent improvement.

Worldwide Coordinated effort and Learning:

The future of modernizing law enforcement stretches out past public boundaries. Teaming up with global accomplices, sharing accepted procedures, and gaining from effective models overall will improve the Indian equity framework. Participating in worldwide discoursed on arising lawful difficulties, mechanical progressions, and basic liberties principles positions India as a proactive member in the worldwide equity scene.

Social Skill and Variety Coordination:

The continuous test of coordinating social skill and variety inside the equity framework requires supported consideration. While progress has been made in perceiving the significance of portrayal, preparing projects, and language access, a ceaseless obligation to these drives is fundamental. Endeavors ought to zero in on encouraging a comprehensive climate that regards and comprehends the different foundations of both lawful experts and the networks they serve.

Estimating and Assessing Effect:

A pivotal part of exploring what's to come is the deliberate estimation and assessment of the effect of drives. Laying out measurements for progress, leading normal effect appraisals, and effectively looking for criticism from partners are fundamental for refining techniques, recognizing regions for development, and guaranteeing that the modernization endeavors line up with the advancing necessities and assumptions for the general public.

Building Public Mindfulness and Trust:

The Lok Sabha's drives to fabricate public mindfulness and trust ought to be a continuous responsibility. Laying out straightforward correspondence channels, demystifying legitimate cycles, and effectively captivating with the general population through different mediums will add to an equity framework that isn't just trusted yet in addition comprehended by the residents it serves.

Flexibility to Cultural Changes:

The flexibility of the law enforcement framework to cultural changes stays a powerful test. Developing normal practices, segment shifts, and social changes require an equity framework that can deftly answer these changes. Nonstop exchange with networks, aversion to developing points of view, and a pledge to equity that mirrors the upsides of contemporary society are fundamental.

Guaranteeing Sufficient Assets:

The supported modernization of the law enforcement framework requires a guarantee to guaranteeing sufficient assets. Asset imperatives can thwart the execution of innovative arrangements, preparing projects, and foundation overhauls. Upholding for spending plan assignments that line up with the scale and significance of modernization drives is fundamental for their prosperity.

9.3 Call to action for continued collaboration and commitment to reform

As we consider the groundbreaking excursion embraced by the Lok Sabha to modernize the law enforcement framework in India, a resonating source of inspiration arises — a call that reverberations past regulative loads, resounding through the passageways of equity, networks, and the shared perspective of society. This call isn't simply an affirmation of past accomplishments however a forward-looking request for supported joint effort, unfaltering responsibility, and a common obligation to explore the intricacies that lie not too far off of improvement in law enforcement.

Embracing a Constant Cooperative Methodology:

The progress of prison regulation on the aggregate endeavors of different partners — administrators, legitimate experts, policing, networks, and mechanical trend-setters. The source of inspiration is an encouragement to embrace a nonstop cooperative methodology, perceiving that the difficulties are multi-layered and request a variety of viewpoints and skill. Gatherings for progressing discourse, associations between legislative bodies and common society, and stages that work with information trade are crucial for supporting energy.

Fortifying Interagency Participation:

A critical part of the source of inspiration is the basic to fortify interagency collaboration. The law enforcement framework is a multifaceted snare of interconnected elements, each assuming a critical part. From policing to the legal executive, from restorative offices to oversight bodies, consistent cooperation is fundamental. Drives that advance data sharing, joint preparation programs, and facilitated reactions to arising difficulties add to a more coordinated and viable law enforcement biological system.

Drawing in with Mechanical Trailblazers:

The fast advancement of innovation requires a continuous commitment with mechanical trend-setters. The source of inspiration welcomes cooperation with specialists in computerized reasoning, information examination, and online protection to guarantee that mechanical arrangements stay at the front of development.

Organizations with research foundations, confidential endeavors, and worldwide innovation pioneers can add to the turn of events and execution of state of the art apparatuses that improve the productivity and reasonableness of the equity framework.

Local area Contribution and Strengthening:

The source of inspiration stresses the centrality of networks in the change cycle. Engaging people group to effectively take part in forming the equity framework cultivates a feeling of pride and shared liability. Local area policing drives, resident warning sheets, and stages for public talk make roads for discourse, understanding, and joint effort. Perceiving the job of networks as partners and accomplices is pivotal for building an equity framework that mirrors the qualities and yearnings of individuals it serves.

Administrative Cautiousness and Responsiveness:

Administrative bodies, especially the Lok Sabha, are called upon to keep up with cautiousness and responsiveness notwithstanding developing difficulties. The source of inspiration highlights the significance of persistently assessing the effect of authoritative changes, adjusting to arising legitimate patterns, and shutting holes in the lawful structure. Proactive commitment with legitimate specialists, scholastic foundations, and worldwide legitimate discussions adds to the refinement of regulations that line up with the standards of equity, common liberties, and worldwide prescribed procedures.

Interest in Preparing and Limit Building:

A powerful law enforcement framework requires a talented and thoroughly prepared labor force. The source of inspiration desires supported interest in preparing and limit working for legitimate experts, cops, and restorative staff. Consistent learning programs that consolidate progressions in legitimate hypothesis, insightful strategies, and mechanical abilities guarantee that the people liable for maintaining equity are prepared to address the difficulties of a unique climate.

Advancing a Culture of Responsibility and Straightforwardness:

Integral to the source of inspiration is the advancement of a culture of responsibility and straightforwardness. Oversight bodies, policing, and legal foundations are called upon to focus on receptiveness in their practices. Laying out instruments for public revealing, leading ordinary reviews, and embracing a culture that invites investigation add to building trust. The source of inspiration supports that responsibility isn't simply an administrative prerequisite yet a natural worth that supports an equitable and fair equity framework.

Adjusting to Worldwide Guidelines and Best Practices:

The source of inspiration advocates for a proactive methodology in adjusting to worldwide principles and best practices. Drawing in with worldwide legitimate gatherings, taking part in cooperative examination tasks, and gaining from fruitful models in different purviews advance the change cycle. Embracing a worldwide viewpoint isn't simply a benchmarking exercise yet an acknowledgment that equity is a common worth that rises above borders.

Compassion and Human-Driven Equity:

At the center of the source of inspiration is an interest for compassion and a human-driven way to deal with equity. Perceiving the lived encounters of people inside the equity framework — be they casualties, wrongdoers, or networks — is fundamental. Supportive equity programs, casualty wrongdoer discoursed, and preventive measures underline an all encompassing comprehension of equity that goes past correctional measures. The source of inspiration welcomes partners to focus on the prosperity, poise, and restoration of people inside the equity framework.

Focusing on Underestimated People group:

The source of inspiration highlights the need to focus on underestimated networks in the change plan. Legitimate guide programs, mindfulness missions, and local area outreach endeavors ought to be designated towards tending to foundational imbalances and guaranteeing that equity is open to all. Perceiving and tending to the interesting difficulties looked by underestimated bunches is a stage towards building an equity framework that is really comprehensive and impartial.

Public Mindfulness Missions:

Supporting the force of change requires continuous public mindfulness crusades. The source of inspiration energizes drives that demystify lawful cycles, teach residents about their privileges, and cultivate a more profound comprehension of the equity framework. Informed residents are enabled residents, and a very much educated public adds to an equity framework that isn't simply powerful however appreciates broad help.

Worldwide Coordinated effort on Arising Difficulties:

Arising difficulties like cybercrime, transnational coordinated wrongdoing, and worldwide security dangers require global joint effort. The source of inspiration welcomes India to effectively draw in with the worldwide local area in tending to these difficulties. Joining peaceful accords, taking part in joint examinations, and teaming up on research drives add to an aggregate reaction that rises above public limits.

Estimating and Imparting Effect:

A fundamental component of the source of inspiration is the obligation to estimating and imparting the effect of change drives. Laying out clear measurements for progress, directing normal assessments, and straightforwardly imparting the results add to public trust. The source of inspiration perceives that influence evaluation isn't simply a regulatory activity yet an exhibition of a promise to responsibility and consistent improvement.

Versatility and Future-Sealing:

The change cycle is a continuous excursion, and the source of inspiration highlights the significance of versatility and future-sealing. Expecting to arise difficulties, embracing creative arrangements, and remaining in front of cultural changes are essential for an equity framework that stays pertinent and viable. The source of inspiration welcomes partners to see change as a powerful cycle that requires dexterity, premonition, and a pledge to remaining at the front of equity development.

Developing a Common Vision:

The source of inspiration is, at its embodiment, a call to develop a common vision of equity — a dream that rises above individual jobs and obligations. It is a dream where equity is certainly not a theoretical idea however a substantial reality that mirrors the qualities, desires, and shared humankind of the different embroidery of Indian culture. Partners are called upon to adjust their endeavors to this common vision, perceiving that the excursion towards a fair and impartial law enforcement framework is an aggregate undertaking.